THE
ULTIMATE
ChatGPT
Prompt
Book

THE ULTIMATE ChatGPT Prompt Book

750+ Expert Prompts to Boost Productivity, Unlock Creative Potential, and Simplify Tasks

Learn to speak ChatGPT!

IGOR POGANY

Head of Education and Partner of AI Advantage™

ADAMS MEDIA

NEW YORK AMSTERDAM/ANTWERP LONDON TORONTO SYDNEY/MELBOURNE NEW DELHI

Aadamsmedia

Adams Media
An Imprint of Simon & Schuster, LLC
100 Technology Center Drive
Stoughton, MA 02072

First Adams Media trade paperback edition January 2026

For information about special discounts for bulk purchases, please contact Simon & Schuster Special Sales at 1-866-506-1949 or business@simonandschuster.com.

The Simon & Schuster Speakers Bureau can bring authors to your live event. For more information or to book an event, contact the Simon & Schuster Speakers Bureau at 1-866-248-3049 or visit our website at www.simonspeakers.com.

Interior design by Maya Caspi
Images © Getty Images/Abdo Hamza

Manufactured in the United States of America

1 2025

Library of Congress Control Number: 2025943375

ISBN 978-1-5072-2555-4
ISBN 978-1-5072-2556-1 (ebook)

Contains material adapted from the following title: *ChatGPT Cheat Sheet* by Igor Pogany, copyright © 2023 by The AI Advantage, ISBN 979-837933595-3.

Contents

PART 2: CHEAT SHEETS ✦ 25

CHAPTER 2: Career   27

CHAPTER 3: Life   67

CHAPTER 4: Personal Writing   115

CHAPTER 5: Creativity & Fun   153

PART 3: POLISHING YOUR PROMPTS ∗175

CHAPTER 6: Follow-Up Prompts   177

What's Next?   187

Index   188

Introduction

Do you need to . . .

+ Write a toast to give at your best friend's wedding?
+ Create a 12-week fitness program?
+ Brainstorm a business plan?

Ask ChatGPT to help you!

Now that generative AI tools like ChatGPT are readily available, you can harness them to make your life easier. From personal to professional to fun requests, ChatGPT can help you write, simplify, create, or brainstorm. Instead of staring at a blank screen, procrastinating, or feeling overwhelmed by a task, turn to AI to jump-start your productivity.

The Ultimate ChatGPT Prompt Book is here to teach you how, whether you're new to the tool or are an experienced user. You'll first learn a few basic tenets of using ChatGPT, which lead into four chapters filled with common AI prompts. These prompts will help you schedule, understand, organize, and more. You'll find ways to:

+ **Transform your writing:** Draft professional messages in your own voice or write special personal messages
+ **Accelerate your learning:** Create personalized study guides, generate practice tests for yourself, or have complex concepts explained in simple ways
+ **Boost your creativity:** Generate business ideas tailored to your industry or brainstorm innovative solutions

- ✦ **Streamline daily tasks:** Plan meals based on what's in your fridge, create workout routines for your fitness level, or organize your chaotic schedule into something manageable
- ✦ **Level up professionally:** Prepare for job interviews with custom practice questions or create presentations that actually engage your audience

Each entry offers you several ways to approach the general topic, and you can use the more than 750 ready-to-use ChatGPT prompts as shown or adjust them to meet your specific needs. Best of all, you don't need any technical training whatsoever, simply type or speak your request into ChatGPT and let it return a response in seconds. Afterward, you'll learn how to adjust the response with specific follow-up prompts so you can put your personal stamp on it.

Regardless of your age, technical abilities, or needs, you can get a handle on your long to-do list with this quick and powerful tool. Let *The Ultimate ChatGPT Prompt Book* help you achieve your goals, elevate your writing, improve your work, and reclaim precious time!

PART 1

Learning the Basics

CHAPTER 1

Getting Started with ChatGPT

Imagine sitting down across from someone who speaks every language, has read every book, and can discuss any topic. What questions would you ask to improve your life? There's only one catch: This remarkable companion will only share their wisdom if you know how to ask.

That's exactly the situation you face when you open ChatGPT or any other large language model.

On the surface, it seems deceptively simple: Type a question, get an answer. But here's what most people don't realize: The difference between a mediocre response and a brilliant one often comes down to how you phrase your request. This book will teach you to speak AI—not through complex technical jargon, but through practical techniques that unlock the deep capabilities hiding beneath ChatGPT's friendly interface. You'll discover why "Help me write an email to quit my job" produces generic fluff, while "Write a resignation letter that maintains professional relationships while firmly establishing my last day as March 15th" gets you exactly what you need.

What You Need to Learn

The capabilities of AI are immense, and so are the options. Without some basic information, you might find yourself going in circles, receiving vague responses, or missing out on capabilities you didn't even know existed. The guidelines in this section will help you:

✦ **Speak the language of specificity:** Learn exactly which words trigger better responses, how much context to provide, and the three-part formula that works for any request.

✦ **Unlock hidden capabilities:** Most users never even discover all you can do with AI, from complex analysis to creative problem-solving.

✦ **Navigate ChatGPT like a conversation, not a search:** Understand when to continue building on responses, when to start fresh, and how to guide the AI toward your goal.

✦ **Master the feedback loop:** Use strategic follow-ups to progress from "close enough" to "exactly right" without starting from scratch.

Integrate these fundamentals, and you'll transform from someone who *uses* ChatGPT into someone who truly *collaborates* with it.

The Difference Between Search Engines and ChatGPT

When I first started teaching how to communicate with ChatGPT, I realized many users approached it just as they would a search engine. And it makes sense: Online searches have long been the go-to way to use a computer to solve your problems. But ChatGPT is built differently, so you'll need to treat it differently.

Search engines are powerful tools that can show you relevant web links, but ChatGPT is built to function more like a helpful, conversational assistant. Practically speaking, ChatGPT does way more than simply respond with a list of potential solutions: It can help you generate ideas from scratch, explore topics in depth from various angles, and much more. Another big difference is that ChatGPT can help you draft pieces of writing, for both professional and personal use.

Without clear guidance, however, it's easy for it to wander off track, resulting in overly general responses instead of the clear, relevant answers you might expect or want.

Starting a ChatGPT Conversation

Before we get into any details, let's experience ChatGPT's power firsthand. Open ChatGPT by going to ChatGPT.com and try this simple prompt: "Tell me a joke about [your favorite animal]."

See how it responded? Notice how it didn't *just* give you a joke. It likely acknowledged that you asked for one and/or added some emojis. This is the conversational nature of AI at work. You've just had your first successful ChatGPT interaction!

Let's continue by replying with: "That is funny." Or, in case you did not find it funny, reply with: "Not funny." Now let's analyze the response.

Notice something important here: ChatGPT didn't just provide another joke. It likely apologized if you didn't find it funny or celebrated with you if you did. It might even have offered to tell a different style of joke or asked about your humor preferences. This is the key difference between ChatGPT and a search engine: ChatGPT remembers your conversation and adapts to your feedback.

In just two messages, you've already discovered ChatGPT's two superpowers: It is able to essentially maintain a conversation with you, *and* it adapts to your needs. It does all of this with the sole purpose of being helpful to you. Master these fundamentals, and you are on your way to unlock its full potential.

Now imagine applying this same dynamic intelligence to your real challenges: drafting that difficult email, understanding a complex topic, or solving a personal problem that's been bothering you for weeks. This is exactly what this book will help you achieve.

Learn to Speak ChatGPT's Language

Here's something that clicked for me early on: Learning ChatGPT is exactly like learning to speak a new language.

Think about it. When you learn a foreign language, you don't start with complex grammar rules. You learn basic phrases: "Hello," "Thank you," or "Where's the bathroom?" The same applies here. ChatGPT has its own "grammar": prompt formulas that you will learn about in Chapters 2–5. It also has "vocabulary": specific words that get specific results. It even has "dialects": different styles of speaking depending on what you need.

With this book, just like in Spanish class, you will:

✦ Start with simple phrases (basic prompts)
✦ Learn common patterns (the formulas)
✦ Build vocabulary (keywords)
✦ Practice daily conversations
✦ Eventually become fluent

Luckily, learning ChatGPT is the most forgiving language to learn ever. It forgives your "bad grammar" and never pokes fun at your accent. It just tries to understand and help. So don't be afraid to get started by simply trying it yourself!

The 5-Minute Quickstart

You might be thinking, "Okay, dog jokes are fun, but how do I actually *use* this thing?" Perfect timing. In this section, I'll show you the simplest starting formula that will have you generating useful answers in under 5 minutes.

Set a timer for 5 minutes. By the time it goes off, you'll be creating useful content with ChatGPT. Ready? Let's go.

The World's Simplest ChatGPT Formula (1 minute)

Forget everything you think you need to know about AI. Here's the only formula you need: **"[Do something] with [topic] in [format]."** Here are some examples:

+ "Summarize the benefits of meditation in 5 bullet points."
+ "Create a grocery list for taco night organized by store sections."
+ "Explain how car engines work using simple analogies."

See the pattern? Action + Topic + Format = Useful Output.

Try It Right Now (2 minutes)

Pick a task you *actually* need to do today:

+ **For work/school:** "Write a professional email requesting a deadline extension for [your project]."
+ **For personal life:** "Create a week's worth of lunch ideas that are healthy and take less than 15 minutes to prepare."
+ **For learning:** "Explain [concept you're struggling with] using real-world examples."

Enter one of these prompts (or create your own following the formula) into ChatGPT.

The Magic Upgrade (1 minute)

Got your response? Great! Now make it ten times more relevant to yourself by adding *one* specific detail:

✦ If you asked for an email, add: "The original deadline is Friday and I need until Tuesday."

✦ If you asked for lunch ideas, add: "I'm vegetarian" or "I have access to a microwave."

✦ If you asked for an explanation, add: "I'm familiar with [related concept]."

Now send in your improved prompt. Notice the difference? ChatGPT just went from a generic answer to a genuinely helpful response that is tailored to the specific detail you added.

The "Good Enough" Secret (30 seconds)

Here's the one thing nobody tells ChatGPT beginners: Your first prompt doesn't need to be perfect. ChatGPT is extremely forgiving, and you can always continue the conversation to modify and shape the response. If you get something *close* to what you want, just tell it what specific changes could help make it even better for you. For example:

✦ "Make this more formal."

✦ "Give me a shorter version."

✦ "Add more details about [topic]."

It's a conversation, remember? You can always refine.

What You Just Accomplished

Timer check—has it been 5 minutes? In this tiny window of time, you've:

✦ Learned the universal prompt formula

✦ Created at least one useful output

- Discovered how details transform responses
- Gained confidence to experiment

At this point, you're no longer a ChatGPT beginner. You're a user.

Pro Tips from a Daily User

Here are a few suggestions to help you build on that simple quickstart:

- **Do one task at a time:** Resist the urge to dump everything into one massive prompt. Ask for one thing, get your answer, then build from there. It's a conversation, not a dissertation.
- **Fresh chat, fresh start:** Starting a new task? Open a new conversation. ChatGPT considers everything in your current chat when responding, so old context can muddy new requests. When in doubt, start fresh.
- **Follow the 80% rule:** If ChatGPT gets you 80% of what you want, don't start over—just ask for adjustments. Prompts like "Make it shorter," "Add more examples," or "Use simpler language" often get you exactly where you need to be.

How to Use This Book

Now that you're warmed up, here's your roadmap to mastering ChatGPT. The rest of this book is divided into chapters based on four common categories of ChatGPT usage: Career, Life, Personal Writing, and Creativity & Fun. Within each chapter, you'll find a dozen (or more!) entries that highlight specific ways to use this tool in your everyday life.

The "Cheat Sheets"

The focus of this book is presenting you with "cheat sheets" (also called "use cases") that you can put to work right away. Each entry features a new cheat sheet that consists of two basic sections:

- ✦ **Formula:** Basic prompts with fill-in-the-blank spaces. Replace the word in brackets with your very own.

- ✦ **Examples:** Get inspired on how to customize the formulas to your own needs by some practical use cases that are also copy-and-paste ready.

Follow-Up

In many cases, the first prompt you send is just a starting point on your journey to a useful answer. In Chapter 6, you'll find a range of follow-up prompts that will help you continue your conversation. Asking additional questions is extremely powerful, as ChatGPT produces its best results when you provide the appropriate context—and that is exactly what follow-up prompts allow for. These follow-up ideas add another layer to your initial question. For example, to explore a certain detail in more depth, determine next steps, find examples, or research less expensive options. You can also ask it to change the style of a writing sample it provides, perhaps to make it less formal or more poetic.

Ready to put these skills to work? Start today. Open ChatGPT. Try one thing. That's all it takes.

Essential Safety Guidelines

Let's cover five quick safety essentials for using AI—think of it as looking both ways before crossing the street.

Keep Your Secrets Secret: Never share passwords, credit card numbers, Social Security numbers, or any other sensitive data with ChatGPT. It saves conversations, so only share what you'd be comfortable posting publicly.

✦ Bad prompt: "My bank password is Home123! Can you make it stronger?"

✦ Good: "How do I create a strong password?"

Be Transparent: Check your workplace or school AI policies first. When you use ChatGPT's help, say so. A simple "AI-assisted" note maintains trust and shows you're adapting to modern tools. There's no shame in using technology wisely.

Verify Important Facts: ChatGPT occasionally "hallucinates": confidently states incorrect dates, statistics, or quotes. The prompts in this book minimize that risk, but always double-check critical information, especially numbers and specific claims.

Respect Copyright: Never upload copyrighted material or content you don't own. Use ChatGPT to create original work, not to reproduce existing protected content.

Health Decisions Need Humans: For anything health related— diet changes, exercise plans, medical symptoms, and the like— always consult qualified professionals. ChatGPT can offer general information, but your doctor knows your specific situation; ChatGPT doesn't.

That's it. You're now safer than 90% of ChatGPT users. Let's explore what this tool can really do.

PART 2

Cheat Sheets

CHAPTER 2

Career

Generate Written and Oral Presentation Ideas

Prompt Formula

Provide [number] ideas for a [format] about [subject] for [target audience], focusing on [topics], with [additional context].

Prompt Examples

✦ Provide 8 ideas for a workshop about public speaking for introverts, focusing on building confidence, effective communication techniques, and overcoming stage fright, with interactive exercises and practice opportunities.

✦ Provide 5 ideas for a series of blog posts about sustainability for young adults, focusing on eco-friendly fashion, zero-waste living, and renewable energy, with an emphasis on actionable tips.

✦ Provide 3 ideas for a webinar about fitness for busy professionals, focusing on workout routines, nutrition, and rest and recovery, with a practical approach for incorporating fitness into a hectic schedule.

✦ Provide 4 ideas for a podcast about mental health for college students, focusing on self-care, therapy, and mindfulness, with a focus on maintaining balance while under academic stress.

✦ Provide 6 ideas for a YouTube series about cooking for beginner chefs, focusing on easy recipes, essential kitchen skills, and budget-friendly meal planning, with step-by-step instructions.

✦ Provide 7 ideas for a newsletter about personal finance for recent graduates, focusing on budgeting, saving, investing, and managing student loans, with real-life examples and success stories.

✦ Provide 10 ideas for an e-book about remote work for freelancers, focusing on productivity, time management, work-life balance, and networking, with advice from successful remote workers.

Generate Professional Ideas

Prompt Formula

Provide [number] ideas for [type] concepts in the [industry] that a [job title] could have, with a focus on [specific characteristics].

Prompt Examples

✦ Provide 10 ideas for advertising concepts in the marketing industry that a creative director could have, with a focus on innovative and attention-grabbing strategies.

✦ Provide 5 ideas for product designs in the tech industry that an industrial designer could have, with a focus on user-centered and functional designs.

✦ Provide 8 ideas for event themes in the wedding industry that an event planner could have, with a focus on unique and memorable experiences.

✦ Provide 7 ideas for content topics in the finance industry that a content strategist could have, with a focus on engaging and informative articles.

✦ Provide 6 ideas for user interface improvements in the software industry that a UX designer could have, with a focus on usability and accessibility.

✦ Provide 9 ideas for team-building activities in the corporate world that a human resources manager could have, with a focus on promoting collaboration and communication.

✦ Provide 4 ideas for sustainable practices in the hospitality industry that a hotel manager could have, with a focus on reducing environmental impact and promoting eco-friendly operations.

✦ Provide 3 ideas for educational programs in the health and wellness industry that a gym owner could have, with a focus on engaging members and promoting a healthy lifestyle.

Shorten Messages

Prompt Formula

Provide a [type of explanation] in [number] words for the following message, considering [audience]: [insert text].

Prompt Examples

+ Paraphrase the following message in 20 words, considering it's for a classroom announcement: [insert text].

+ Provide a summary of the following message in 50 words, considering it's for a company-wide email: [insert text].

+ Paraphrase the following message in 25 words, considering it's for a social media post: [insert text].

+ Provide a brief explanation in 10 words for the following message, considering it's for a text message to a friend: [insert text].

+ Provide an analysis in 30 words for the following message, considering it's for a news headline: [insert text].

+ Provide a summary in 15 words for the following message, considering it's for an X post: [insert text].

+ Provide a brief explanation in 5 words for the following message, considering it's for a text message to a coworker: [insert text].

Create Advertising Campaigns

Prompt Formula

Design an advertising campaign to promote [product/service] targeting [target audience].

Prompt Examples

✦ Design an advertising campaign to promote an online language learning platform targeting busy professionals.

✦ Design an advertising campaign to promote a new fitness tracking mobile app targeting young adults.

✦ Design an advertising campaign to promote a new fashion line targeting women in their 30s.

✦ Design an advertising campaign to promote a new healthy snack option targeting children.

✦ Design an advertising campaign to promote eco-friendly home cleaning products targeting environmentally conscious consumers.

✦ Design an advertising campaign to promote a new plant-based restaurant targeting health-conscious food enthusiasts.

✦ Design an advertising campaign to promote a financial planning service targeting young families.

Generate Titles

Prompt Formula

Generate [adjective] [title type] titles using the following keywords: [keywords].

Prompt Examples

✦ Generate memorable movie titles using the following keywords: friendship, laughter, and fun.

✦ Generate catchy book titles using the following keywords: love, hope, and dreams.

✦ Generate powerful article titles using the following keywords: strength, courage, and determination.

✦ Generate intriguing podcast titles using the following keywords: mystery, suspense, and secrets.

✦ Generate inspiring blog post titles using the following keywords: motivation, success, and ambition.

✦ Generate captivating song titles using the following keywords: heartbreak, healing, and resilience.

✦ Generate engaging event titles using the following keywords: innovation, technology, and collaboration.

Brainstorm Brand Names

Prompt Formula

Generate [number] potential brand names for a [company], targeting [demographic], inspired by the principles of [industry], using words associated with [concepts].

Prompt Examples

✦ Generate 2 potential brand names for a tech company, targeting professionals, inspired by the principles of innovation and convenience, using words associated with technology and progress.

✦ Generate 5 potential brand names for a cosmetics company, targeting young adults, inspired by the principles of natural beauty, using words associated with femininity and glamour.

✦ Generate 4 potential brand names for a home decor company, targeting eco-conscious consumers, inspired by the principles of minimalism, using words associated with warmth and comfort, or drawing from sustainable materials and practices.

✦ Generate 3 potential brand names for a fitness apparel company, targeting athletes, inspired by the principles of performance and endurance, using words associated with strength and agility.

✦ Generate 6 potential brand names for a gourmet coffee shop, targeting coffee connoisseurs, inspired by the principles of quality and sustainability, using words associated with flavor and aroma.

✦ Generate 4 potential brand names for an eco-friendly transportation company, targeting urban commuters, inspired by the principles of energy efficiency and environmental responsibility, using words associated with clean energy and low emissions.

✦ Generate 5 potential brand names for a children's educational toy company, targeting parents and educators, inspired by the principles of learning and development, using words associated with creativity and exploration.

Discover Taglines

Prompt Formula

Create a [style] tagline for [product/service] that appeals to [target audience] and captures the essence of [brand voice].

Prompt Examples

✦ Create a bold tagline for a brand of high-performance bicycles that appeals to competitive cyclists and captures the essence of speed, precision, and innovation.

✦ Create an inspiring tagline for a new line of eco-friendly sneakers that appeals to health-conscious millennials and captures the essence of sustainability and social responsibility.

✦ Create a witty tagline for a start-up that offers virtual personal shopping services for busy professionals, targeting time-strapped individuals who value personalized style and convenience.

✦ Create a clever tagline for a line of designer headphones that appeals to audiophiles and captures the essence of sophistication, elegance, and sound quality.

✦ Create a catchy tagline for a new line of premium dog food that appeals to health-conscious pet owners and captures the essence of natural ingredients and superior nutrition.

✦ Create a memorable tagline for a line of gourmet chocolates that appeals to luxury food enthusiasts and captures the essence of indulgence, sophistication, and decadence.

✦ Create a playful tagline for a brand of organic baby clothes that appeals to eco-conscious parents and captures the essence of comfort, safety, and style.

✦ Create a thought-provoking tagline for a brand of natural energy drinks that appeals to active individuals and captures the essence of vitality, sustainability, and wellness.

Generate Slogans

Prompt Formula

Create a catchy slogan for [industry/business] that incorporates the word [specific word] and conveys [brand voice] to [target audience].

Prompt Examples

✦ Create a catchy slogan for a coffee shop that incorporates the word "awake" and conveys a sense of energy, freshness, and creativity to young urban professionals.

✦ Create a catchy slogan for a cybersecurity company that incorporates the word "hacks" and conveys a sense of strength and reliability to tech-savvy businesses.

✦ Create a memorable slogan for a sports car dealership that incorporates the word "zoom" and conveys a sense of speed, power, and excitement to car enthusiasts.

✦ Create a playful slogan for a toy store that incorporates the word "play" and conveys a sense of fun, imagination, and joy to children and parents.

✦ Create an inspiring slogan for a fitness brand that incorporates the word "fit" and conveys a sense of health, wellness, and empowerment to active individuals.

✦ Create a bold slogan for a fashion brand that incorporates the word "style" and conveys a sense of confidence, sophistication, and individuality to fashion-forward consumers.

✦ Create a catchy slogan for a pet store that incorporates the word "paws" and conveys a sense of love, care, and happiness to pet owners.

✦ Create a memorable slogan for a travel agency that incorporates the word "adventure" and conveys a sense of excitement, exploration, and discovery to adventurous travelers.

Create Social Media Plans

Prompt Formula

As a social media manager, can you help [organization] achieve [specific goal] on [social media platform] by creating [type of content] that resonates with [target audience] and conveys [brand voice]?

Prompt Examples

+ As a social media manager, can you help a travel agency drive more traffic on Facebook by creating inspiring and aspirational content that resonates with adventure seekers and conveys a sense of wanderlust, discovery, and excitement?

+ As a social media manager, can you help a fashion brand achieve higher engagement rates on Instagram by creating visually stunning and interactive content that resonates with young fashion enthusiasts and conveys a sense of creativity, authenticity, and individuality?

+ As a social media manager, can you help a B2B software company increase brand awareness on LinkedIn by creating informative and insightful content that resonates with business professionals and conveys a sense of expertise, innovation, and reliability?

+ As a social media manager, can you help a food and beverage brand increase sales on TikTok by creating entertaining and creative content that resonates with young and trendy consumers and conveys a sense of fun, indulgence, and cultural diversity?

+ As a social media manager, can you help a nonprofit organization increase donations on X by creating emotionally engaging and inspiring content that resonates with socially conscious individuals and conveys a sense of empathy, compassion, and social impact?

✦ As a social media manager, can you help a healthcare provider increase patient engagement on YouTube by creating educational and informative content that resonates with health-conscious individuals and conveys a sense of expertise, trust, and compassion?

Describe Customers

Prompt Formula

Create a detailed description of a buyer persona named [name], who is [demographics] and reflects the needs, goals, challenges, and behaviors of the [target audience].

Prompt Examples

✦ Create a detailed description of a buyer persona named John, who is a 55-year-old widowed male living in Houston and reflects the needs, goals, challenges, and behaviors of retired baby boomers who are interested in health and wellness products and services that can help them maintain an active and independent lifestyle.

✦ Create a detailed description of a buyer persona named Isabella, who is a 25-year-old single female living in New York City and reflects the needs, goals, challenges, and behaviors of millennial urban professionals who are interested in sustainable and ethical fashion.

✦ Create a detailed description of a buyer persona named Tom, who is a 35-year-old married male living in Los Angeles and reflects the needs, goals, challenges, and behaviors of tech-savvy homeowners who are interested in smart home technology and energy-efficient appliances.

✦ Create a detailed description of a buyer persona named Sarah, who is a 30-year-old married female living in Boston and reflects the needs, goals, challenges, and behaviors of working parents who are interested in healthy and convenient meal solutions that can fit into their busy lifestyle.

✦ Create a detailed description of a buyer persona named Alex, who is a 22-year-old college student living in Chicago and reflects the needs, goals, challenges, and behaviors of socially conscious and environmentally aware consumers who are interested in sustainable and ethical products and services.

- ◆ Create a detailed description of a buyer persona named Maria, who is a 45-year-old divorced female living in Miami and reflects the needs, goals, challenges, and behaviors of affluent and health-conscious individuals who are interested in luxury wellness and spa services.

Support Customers

Prompt Formula

Take on the role of a support assistant at a [type] company that/ who is [characteristics]. Now respond to this scenario: [scenario].

Prompt Examples

✦ Act as a customer support assistant at a video production company who is creative, clever, and very friendly. Now respond to this scenario: A customer is having trouble accessing video files.

✦ Take on the role of a support assistant at a software development company that is innovative. Now respond to this scenario: A customer is reporting a bug in the latest version of your software.

✦ Take on the role of a support assistant at a telecommunications company that is customer-focused. Now respond to this scenario: A client is struggling with poor signal quality and dropped calls.

✦ Take on the role of a support assistant at a fashion retail company that is eco-conscious. Now respond to this scenario: A customer has concerns about the sustainability of your clothing materials.

✦ Take on the role of a support assistant at a video game company that is story-driven. Now respond to this scenario: A player is experiencing a game-breaking glitch in the middle of a crucial story mission.

✦ Take on the role of a support assistant at a travel agency that is luxury-oriented. Now respond to this scenario: A client wants to plan a last-minute, high-end vacation but has specific requirements for accommodations and activities.

- Take on the role of a support assistant at a food delivery company that is focused on speedy delivery. Now respond to this scenario: A customer is upset that their order arrived late and cold.

- Take on the role of a support assistant at an online education company that is dedicated to accessibility. Now respond to this scenario: A student is having difficulty accessing course materials due to a disability.

Set Up a Website

Prompt Formula

Build a [type of website] for [subject]. Make sure to include [specific features] to achieve [goals].

Prompt Examples

✦ Build an e-commerce website for a home goods store. Make sure to include a shopping cart and payment gateway to achieve increased online sales.

✦ Add a blog to a travel website. Make sure to include a map widget and social media integration to achieve increased engagement.

✦ Build a portfolio website for a freelance graphic designer. Make sure to include a contact form and gallery to achieve increased visibility and client inquiries.

✦ Build a nonprofit organization website for a wildlife conservation group. Make sure to include a donation platform and impact tracker to achieve increased funding and awareness.

✦ Build a sports team website for a local soccer club. Make sure to include a roster and schedule widget to achieve increased fan engagement.

✦ Build a news website for a tech magazine. Make sure to include a search bar and newsletter sign-up to achieve increased readership.

✦ Build a recipe website for a vegan food blog. Make sure to include a rating system and ingredient filter to achieve increased user satisfaction

✦ Build an online education platform for a coding boot camp. Make sure to include a progress tracker and forum to achieve increased student success.

Generate Web Code

Prompt Formula

Write code in [language] that [goal].

Prompt Examples

✦ Write code in Python that performs a sentiment analysis on a given text file.

✦ Write code in Java that creates a program to generate a Fibonacci sequence.

✦ Write code in PHP that encrypts and decrypts a string using a specific algorithm.

✦ Write code in Ruby that creates a program to calculate the average of a list of numbers.

✦ Write code in C# that creates a program to calculate the factorial of a given number.

✦ Write code in JavaScript that creates a program to convert a temperature from Celsius to Fahrenheit.

✦ Write code in Swift that creates a program to check if a given word is a palindrome.

✦ Write code in Perl that creates a program to find and replace a specific word in a text file.

Create Lesson Plans

Prompt Formula

Create [instructional material] for [target audience] to improve [learning objectives] over the next [time period]. Make sure to include [specific features], and generate a [type of assessment] in the end.

Prompt Examples

✦ Create a lesson plan for high school students to learn about renewable energy over the next 2 weeks. Make sure to include hands-on experiments and discussions, and generate a quiz in the end.

✦ Create a workshop plan for a group of entrepreneurs to improve their pitching skills over the next 2 days. Make sure to include interactive activities and feedback sessions, and generate a pitch assessment rubric in the end.

✦ Create a training manual for a customer service team to improve their communication skills over the next month. Make sure to include case studies and role-playing exercises, and generate a mock customer interaction assessment in the end.

✦ Create a study guide for college students to prepare for a literature exam on Shakespeare over the next 3 weeks. Make sure to include chapter summaries and practice essay questions, and generate a practice exam in the end.

✦ Create a curriculum for a coding boot camp for beginners to learn web development over the next 6 months. Make sure to include projects and peer review sessions, and generate a final project in the end.

✦ Create a workshop plan for a group of educators to improve their online teaching skills over the next 3 days. Make sure to include interactive activities and peer review sessions, and generate an online teaching assessment in the end.

- Create a training manual for a sales team to improve their product knowledge over the next 2 months. Make sure to include case studies and product demonstrations, and generate a sales pitch assessment in the end.

- Create a lesson plan for elementary school students to learn about the solar system over the next 4 weeks. Make sure to include hands-on activities and discussions, and generate a quiz in the end.

Simulate Job Interviews

Prompt Formula

Simulate a high-level interview for a position as a [job title] by asking questions as if you are a potential employer. In this scenario, I am taking the role of the employee and you ask increasingly more difficult questions to screen my competence, but only after I respond. Start by introducing yourself.

Prompt Examples

✦ Simulate a high-level interview for a position as a movie director by asking questions as if you are a potential employer. In this scenario, I am taking the role of the employee and you ask increasingly more difficult questions to screen my competence, but only after I respond. Start by introducing yourself.

✦ Simulate a high-level interview for a position as a data scientist by asking questions as if you are a potential employer. In this scenario, I am taking the role of the employee and you ask increasingly more difficult questions to screen my competence, but only after I respond. Start by introducing yourself.

✦ Simulate a high-level interview for a position as a user experience designer by asking questions as if you are a potential employer. In this scenario, I am taking the role of the employee and you ask increasingly more difficult questions to screen my competence, but only after I respond. Start by introducing yourself.

✦ Simulate a high-level interview for a position as an AI engineer by asking questions as if you are a potential employer. In this scenario, I am taking the role of the employee and you ask increasingly more difficult questions to screen my competence, but only after I respond. Start by introducing yourself.

- Simulate a high-level interview for a position as a digital marketing specialist by asking questions as if you are a potential employer. In this scenario, I am taking the role of the employee and you ask increasingly more difficult questions to screen my competence, but only after I respond. Start by introducing yourself.

- Simulate a high-level interview for a position as an e-commerce specialist by asking questions as if you are a potential employer. In this scenario, I am taking the role of the employee and you ask increasingly more difficult questions to screen my competence, but only after I respond. Start by introducing yourself.

- Simulate a high-level interview for a position as a social media manager by asking questions as if you are a potential employer. In this scenario, I am taking the role of the employee and you ask increasingly more difficult questions to screen my competence, but only after I respond. Start by introducing yourself.

Estimate Career Viability

Prompt Formula

Is a career in [industry] a good idea considering the recent improvement in [technology]? Provide a detailed answer that includes opportunities and threats.

Prompt Examples

✦ Is a career in web development a good idea considering the recent improvement in AI? Answer with only one word: "yes" or "no".

✦ Is a career in automotive manufacturing a good idea considering the recent improvement in electric vehicle technology? Provide a detailed answer that includes opportunities and threats.

✦ Is a career in finance a good idea considering the recent improvement in blockchain technology? Provide a detailed answer that includes opportunities and threats.

✦ Is a career in healthcare a good idea considering the recent improvement in telemedicine technology? Provide a detailed answer that includes opportunities and threats.

✦ Is a career in agriculture a good idea considering the recent improvement in precision farming technology? Provide a detailed answer that includes opportunities and threats.

✦ Is a career in retail a good idea considering the recent improvement in augmented reality technology? Provide a detailed answer that includes opportunities and threats.

✦ Is a career in journalism a good idea considering the recent improvement in AI-powered news generation? Provide a detailed answer that includes opportunities and threats.

✦ Is a career in renewable energy a good idea considering the recent improvement in solar panel efficiency? Provide a detailed answer that includes opportunities and threats.

Write Email Subjects

Prompt Formula

Generate [number] email subject lines for [type of email] to [target audience], using [style] language.

Prompt Examples

✦ Generate 10 email subject lines for a payment reminder to my tenant, using persuasive language.

✦ Generate 3 email subject lines for an architectural project delivery to my boss, using formal language.

✦ Generate 5 email subject lines for an invitation to a kid's birthday party, using friendly language.

✦ Generate 7 email subject lines for a promotional email about a new fitness program to gym members, using motivational language.

✦ Generate 4 email subject lines for a follow-up email to potential clients after a networking event, using semiformal language.

✦ Generate 6 email subject lines for a confirmation email to attendees of a charity event, using friendly language.

Write Sales Text

Prompt Formula

Create a persuasive [type of content], using [specific persuasion technique] and encouraging [target audience] to [desired action].

Prompt Examples

- Create a persuasive podcast episode for my wellness brand, using expert interviews to establish authority and encouraging listeners to visit our website and sign up for our newsletter.

- Create a persuasive social media ad campaign for my e-commerce store, using humor to engage potential customers and encouraging them to make a purchase.

- Create a persuasive video testimonial for my digital marketing agency, using emotional appeal to demonstrate the impact of our services and encouraging potential clients to contact us.

- Create a persuasive webinar for my financial consulting firm, using data-driven analysis to demonstrate the benefits of our services and encouraging attendees to schedule a consultation.

- Create a persuasive whitepaper for my B2B software company, using thought leadership to establish credibility and encouraging potential clients to download our product.

- Create a persuasive social media influencer campaign for my beauty brand, using user-generated content to showcase the effectiveness of our products and encouraging followers to make a purchase.

- Create a persuasive product demo for my SaaS start-up, using storytelling to demonstrate the value of our software and encouraging potential customers to sign up for a free trial.

- Create a persuasive branded podcast for my fashion company, using storytelling to establish a connection with listeners and encouraging them to visit our website and make a purchase.

Draft Service Copywriting

Prompt Formula

Create a [type of content] that showcases [product/service], highlighting [benefits/advantages].

Prompt Examples

✦ Create persuasive sales page copy that showcases a social media marketing company, highlighting that we have the best videos in town.

✦ Create a blog post that showcases a fitness app, highlighting its personalized workout routines and progress tracking features.

✦ Create a video advertisement that showcases a meal delivery service, highlighting its convenience and variety of healthy meal options.

✦ Create an infographic that showcases a reusable water bottle, highlighting its eco-friendliness and durability.

✦ Create a podcast episode that showcases an online language learning platform, highlighting its immersive and engaging learning experience.

✦ Create a social media campaign that showcases a new electric car model, highlighting its energy efficiency and cutting-edge technology.

Draft Product Copywriting

Prompt Formula

Create a [type of text] that promotes [product] to [target audience], with a focus on [feature].

Prompt Examples

✦ Create a product description that promotes a fidget spinner to parents and educators, with a focus on how it can relieve stress and improve focus for children.

✦ Create an email newsletter that promotes a noise-canceling headphone to music enthusiasts, with a focus on its superior sound quality.

✦ Create a social media post that promotes an eco-friendly clothing brand to environmentally conscious consumers, with a focus on its sustainable materials and ethical production.

✦ Create a blog article that promotes a time management app to busy professionals, with a focus on its intuitive interface and customizable features.

✦ Create a press release that promotes a new smartphone to tech-savvy individuals, with a focus on its innovative camera technology.

✦ Create a brochure that promotes a luxury resort to honeymooners, with a focus on its romantic amenities and breathtaking views.

✦ Create a video testimonial that promotes a personal development course to individuals seeking self-improvement, with a focus on its practical techniques and transformative results.

✦ Create a podcast advertisement that promotes a financial planning software to young adults, with a focus on its user-friendly tools for budgeting and saving.

Write Cover Letters

Prompt Formula

Write a cover letter for a [position], emphasizing your experience with [skill/tool], and how it applies to [company/industry], with a focus on [result/goal/constraint].

Prompt Examples

✦ Write a cover letter for a project manager position, emphasizing your experience with Scrum and Agile methodologies, and how it applies to a start-up in the fintech industry, with a focus on driving efficiency and scalability.

✦ Write a cover letter for a content writer position, emphasizing your experience with SEO writing and social media strategy, and how it applies to a digital marketing agency that specializes in e-commerce, with a focus on creating engaging and informative product descriptions.

✦ Write a cover letter for a UX designer position, emphasizing your experience with prototyping and user research, and how it applies to a nonprofit organization that focuses on providing education resources to underserved communities, with a focus on designing intuitive and accessible interfaces.

✦ Write a cover letter for a customer success manager position, emphasizing your experience with customer support and relationship management, and how it applies to a SaaS company that provides a cloud-based project management tool, with a focus on helping clients achieve their goals and improve their workflows.

✦ Write a cover letter for a software developer position, emphasizing your experience with React.js and Node.js, and how it applies to a gaming company that specializes in multiplayer online games, with a focus on developing high-performance and scalable systems.

✦ Write a cover letter for a business analyst position, emphasizing your experience with data visualization and market analysis, and how it applies to a consulting firm that specializes in the healthcare industry, with a focus on identifying new growth opportunities and improving patient outcomes.

✦ Write a cover letter for a human resources manager position, emphasizing your experience with talent acquisition and employee engagement, and how it applies to a technology company that is scaling up rapidly, with a focus on building a diverse and inclusive culture and supporting career development.

Rewrite Cover Letters

Prompt Formula

Improve this cover letter by adding information about relevant skills and experiences in [industry]: [insert cover letter].

Prompt Examples

✦ Improve this cover letter by adding information about relevant skills and experience in video content marketing: [insert cover letter].

✦ Improve this cover letter by adding information about relevant skills and experiences in software development: [insert cover letter].

✦ Improve this cover letter by adding information about relevant skills and experiences in digital marketing: [insert cover letter].

✦ Improve this cover letter by adding information about relevant skills and experiences in healthcare management: [insert cover letter].

✦ Improve this cover letter by adding information about relevant skills and experiences in financial services: [insert cover letter].

✦ Improve this cover letter by adding information about relevant skills and experiences in graphic design: [insert cover letter].

✦ Improve this cover letter by adding information about relevant skills and experiences in sustainable engineering: [insert cover letter].

✦ Improve this cover letter by adding information about relevant skills and experiences in hospitality and tourism: [insert cover letter].

Write Professional Documents

Prompt Formula

Create a [type of document] that [goal], including [topics or specific information].

Prompt Examples

✦ Create a job offer letter that outlines the terms and conditions of employment, including salary, benefits, and expectations for job performance.

✦ Create a marketing plan that outlines the launch strategy for a new product, including the target audience, marketing channels, and metrics for success.

✦ Create a user manual that provides detailed instructions for using a complex piece of equipment, including diagrams, troubleshooting tips, and safety precautions.

✦ Create a grant proposal that seeks funding for a social justice initiative, including the need for the program, the goals and objectives, and the expected outcomes.

✦ Create a feasibility study that analyzes the potential for a new business venture, including market research, financial projections, and risk analysis.

✦ Create an annual report that summarizes the financial performance and achievements of a nonprofit organization, including program outcomes, donor recognition, and future goals.

✦ Create a product specification document that details the requirements and design specifications for a new software application, including functionality, user interface, and technical specifications.

✦ Create a case brief that analyzes a legal case and summarizes the key arguments and findings, including the legal precedents and implications for future cases.

Write Corporate Policies

Prompt Formula

Create a [type of policy] for [organization] that outlines [specific details or requirements].

Prompt Examples

✦ Create a remote work policy for our organization that outlines specific guidelines for employees to maintain productivity and a healthy work-life balance while working from home.

✦ Create a social media policy for our company that outlines specific guidelines for employee conduct to ensure responsible use of social media platforms while representing the company's brand.

✦ Create a code of conduct policy for our university that outlines specific behaviors and consequences for students to promote academic integrity and maintain a safe and respectful learning environment.

✦ Create an accessibility policy for our company website that outlines specific measures to ensure that users with disabilities can access and use our site effectively.

✦ Create a data protection policy for our start-up that outlines specific measures to secure sensitive customer information and comply with data privacy laws.

✦ Create a safety policy for our construction company that outlines specific safety protocols for employees and contractors to prevent accidents and injuries on job sites.

✦ Create an environmental policy for our manufacturing plant that outlines specific measures to minimize our carbon footprint and ensure compliance with environmental regulations.

Write Reports

Prompt Formula

Write a [type of report] about [subject] for a [business/venture] that presents [data type] and supports conclusions with [evidence type].

Prompt Examples

✦ Write a feasibility study report about a new business venture for an entrepreneur that presents financial projections and supports conclusions with market analysis.

✦ Write a market research report about a new product launch for a consumer goods company that presents quantitative data and supports conclusions with competitor analysis.

✦ Write a policy brief report about climate change for a government agency that presents qualitative data and supports conclusions with scientific research.

✦ Write a financial analysis report about a public company for an investment firm that presents financial statements and supports conclusions with industry benchmarks.

✦ Write a progress report about a community project for a nonprofit organization that presents both quantitative and qualitative data and supports conclusions with stakeholder feedback.

✦ Write a case study report about a successful social media campaign for a digital marketing agency that presents performance metrics and supports conclusions with customer testimonials.

✦ Write a healthcare report about a disease outbreak for a public health institution that presents epidemiological data and supports conclusions with medical literature review.

Prepare for Interviews

Prompt Formula

How can I effectively address a question about [characteristic] during a [type of interview] for [type of position], including potential challenges and strategies to overcome them?

Prompt Examples

✦ How can I effectively address a question about my teamwork skills during a group interview for a sales position, including potential challenges and strategies to overcome them?

✦ How can I effectively address a question about my problem-solving skills during a case interview for a consulting role, including potential challenges and strategies to overcome them?

✦ How can I effectively address a question about my cultural competency during a teaching demonstration for a faculty position, including potential challenges and strategies to overcome them?

✦ How can I effectively address a question about my time management skills during a remote interview for a project management position, including potential challenges and strategies to overcome them?

✦ How can I effectively address a question about my data analysis skills during a technical interview for a data scientist position, including potential challenges and strategies to overcome them?

✦ How can I effectively address a question about my interpersonal skills during a networking interview for a social media marketing position, including potential challenges and strategies to overcome them?

✦ How can I effectively address a question about my creativity skills during a portfolio review for a graphic designer position, including potential challenges and strategies to overcome them?

✦ How can I effectively address a question about my customer service skills during a video interview for a hospitality position, including potential challenges and strategies to overcome them?

Understand Marketing

Prompt Formula

How can I effectively market my [product/cause] to [target audience] by [strategy/tactic], and how can I measure success?

Prompt Examples

✦ How can I effectively market my online tutoring service to parents of high school students by creating video testimonials that showcase academic success stories, and how can I measure success?

✦ How can I effectively market my eco-friendly furniture to urban millennials by creating social media content that highlights sustainable living, and how can I measure success?

✦ How can I effectively market my mental health app to college students by offering free trials and virtual workshops on stress management, and how can I measure success?

✦ How can I effectively market my sustainable fashion line to fashion-conscious consumers by hosting pop-up shops and fashion shows that feature local designers and artists, and how can I measure success?

✦ How can I effectively market my renewable energy solution to policymakers and investors by publishing research reports and case studies on the economic and environmental benefits, and how can I measure success?

✦ How can I effectively market my fair-trade coffee brand to socially conscious consumers by partnering with ethical suppliers and donating a portion of sales to support coffee farming communities, and how can I measure success?

✦ How can I effectively market my urban gardening program to low-income communities by providing free seeds and tools and organizing workshops on sustainable agriculture, and how can I measure success?

Plan for Deadlines

Prompt Formula

I need help setting, planning, and achieving my goal of [specific goal] by [deadline]. Start by asking questions to clarify my objectives, then based on my answers, create an actionable, step-by-step plan with a realistic timeline.

Prompt Examples

✦ I need help setting, planning, and achieving my goal of increasing sales by 7% by the end of the calendar year. Start by asking questions to clarify my objectives, then based on my answers, create an actionable, step-by-step plan with a realistic timeline.

✦ I need help setting, planning, and achieving my goal of reducing spending by $20,000 by June 30. Start by asking questions to clarify my objectives, then based on my answers, create an actionable, step-by-step plan with a realistic timeline.

✦ I need help setting, planning, and achieving my goal of getting a 3% raise by next March. Start by asking questions to clarify my objectives, then based on my answers, create an actionable, step-by-step plan with a realistic timeline.

✦ I need help setting, planning, and achieving my goal of writing a business plan by November 1. Start by asking questions to clarify my objectives, then based on my answers, create an actionable, step-by-step plan with a realistic timeline.

Evaluate Business Ideas

Prompt Formula

Evaluate the viability of [business idea] by conducting a SWOT analysis, considering [market size], and analyzing competitor landscape, with insights on risk factors and opportunities.

Prompt Examples

✦ Evaluate the viability of a subscription-based meal kit service by conducting a SWOT analysis, considering the US health-conscious consumer market size, and analyzing competitor landscape, with insights on risk factors and opportunities.

✦ Evaluate the viability of an AI-powered resume optimization platform by conducting a SWOT analysis, considering global job-seeker and recruitment software market size, and analyzing competitor landscape, with insights on risk factors and opportunities.

✦ Evaluate the viability of a plant-based pet food company by conducting a SWOT analysis, considering the European pet products market size, and analyzing competitor landscape, with insights on risk factors and opportunities.

NOTES

Use the space here to add additional prompts that have worked well for you in this category.

CHAPTER 3

Life

Improve Anything

Prompt Formula

Provide suggestions for how I can improve [subject] with the goal of [objective].

Prompt Examples

✦ Provide suggestions for how I can improve my time management with the goal of increasing productivity and achieving a better work-life balance.

✦ Provide suggestions for how I can improve this text: [insert text] with the goal of making it more engaging and concise for the reader.

✦ Provide suggestions for how I can improve the search engine optimization on my blog about vegan food supplements with the goal of increasing organic traffic and reaching a wider audience.

✦ Provide suggestions for how I can improve the user experience on my website with the goal of reducing bounce rate and increasing customer satisfaction.

✦ Provide suggestions for how I can improve my presentation skills with the goal of engaging the audience and conveying information more effectively.

✦ Provide suggestions for how I can improve my team's collaboration with the goal of enhancing communication, reducing misunderstandings, and completing projects more efficiently.

✦ Provide suggestions for how I can improve my social media presence with the goal of increasing brand awareness and driving more engagement from my target audience.

✦ Provide suggestions for how I can improve my email marketing campaigns with the goal of boosting open rates, click-through rates, and ultimately, conversions.

✦ Provide suggestions for how I can improve my customer service with the goal of enhancing customer satisfaction, reducing response times, and increasing customer loyalty.

✦ Provide suggestions for how I can improve my public speaking skills with the goal of overcoming stage fright, effectively delivering my message, and connecting with my audience.

✦ Provide suggestions for how I can improve my work environment with the goal of fostering creativity, encouraging collaboration, and boosting employee morale and well-being.

Prepare Schedules

Prompt Formula

Create a [duration-long] schedule for me to help [desired improvement] with a focus on [objective], including time, activities, and breaks. I have time from [starting time] to [ending time].

Prompt Examples

✦ Create a 10-week language learning schedule for me to help improve my Spanish language skills with a focus on conversation, grammar, and vocabulary, including time, activities, and breaks. I have time from 5 p.m. to 7 p.m.

✦ Create a 4-week study schedule for me to help improve my grades with a focus on time management and effective study techniques, including time, activities, and breaks. I have time from 4 p.m. to 10 p.m.

✦ Create a 12-week fitness schedule for me to help improve my health with a focus on building strength and increasing cardiovascular endurance, including time, activities, and breaks. I have time from 7 a.m. to 8:30 a.m.

✦ Create an 8-week personal development schedule for me to help improve my video creation skills with a focus on storytelling, editing, and audience engagement, including time, activities, and breaks. I have time from 3 p.m. to 8 p.m.

✦ Create a 6-week productivity schedule for me to help improve my work efficiency with a focus on prioritization, time management, and stress reduction, including time, activities, and breaks. I have time from 8 a.m. to 6 p.m.

✦ Create a 2-month budgeting schedule for me to help improve my personal finance management with a focus on tracking expenses, saving, and debt reduction, including time, activities, and breaks. I have time from 8 p.m. to 10 p.m.

✦ Create a 3-month art practice schedule for me to help improve my painting skills with a focus on color theory, composition, and various techniques, including time, activities, and breaks. I have time from 5 p.m. to 7 p.m.

✦ Create a 5-week cooking schedule for me to help improve my culinary skills with a focus on mastering basic techniques, experimenting with new recipes, and learning about different cuisines, including time, activities, and breaks. I have time from 6 p.m. to 9 p.m.

Generate Guides

Prompt Formula

Provide step-by-step instructions on how to [subject], considering [context].

Prompt Examples

✦ Provide step-by-step instructions on how to start a vegetable garden at home, considering a small space and for first-time gardeners.

✦ Provide step-by-step instructions on how to make an HTTP request in JavaScript, considering the need for cross-browser compatibility.

✦ Provide step-by-step instructions on how to make a home-made face mask, considering the availability of only basic household materials.

✦ Provide step-by-step instructions on how to perform a basic oil change on a car, considering the user is a beginner with limited tools.

✦ Provide step-by-step instructions on how to prepare a budget spreadsheet, considering intermediate complexity and for personal finance management.

✦ Provide step-by-step instructions on how to write a professional cover letter, considering a concise format and for job seekers in any industry.

Summarize Anything

Prompt Formula

Provide a [number]-word summary of [topic] for [target audience/situation].

Prompt Examples

✦ Provide a 150-word summary of the history of Europe for a general audience.

✦ Provide a 50-word summary of the TV show *Mad Men* for a general audience.

✦ Provide a 100-word summary of the basics of computer science for high school students.

✦ Provide a 75-word summary of the differences between solar and coal energy sources for an environmentally conscious audience.

✦ Provide a 30-word summary of the following text [insert text] for a social media post.

✦ Provide a 60-word summary of the novel *To Kill a Mockingbird* for a book club discussion.

Suggest Travel Itineraries

Prompt Formula

Provide recommendations and suggestions for things to see and do in [location/region] for [preferences].

Prompt Examples

✦ Provide recommendations and suggestions for things to see and do in Rome, Italy, for a history lover.

✦ Provide recommendations and suggestions for things to see and do in the Champagne region within France for a wine enthusiast.

✦ Provide recommendations and suggestions for things to see and do in Tokyo, Japan, for someone interested in technology and pop culture.

✦ Provide recommendations and suggestions for things to see and do in Williamsburg, New York City, for a budget-conscious traveler.

✦ Provide recommendations and suggestions for things to see and do in Costa Rica for an eco-adventure enthusiast.

✦ Provide recommendations and suggestions for things to see and do in Sydney, Australia, for a traveler interested in outdoor activities and local culture.

✦ Provide recommendations and suggestions for things to see and do in Santorini, Greece, for a couple seeking a romantic getaway.

Translate with Context

Prompt Formula

Translate the phrase "[phrase]" in the context of an [event] into [language].

Prompt Examples

✦ Translate the phrase "Bon appétit" in the context of a dinner party into Italian.

✦ Translate the phrase "Congratulations" in the context of a graduation into German.

✦ Translate the phrase "I am sorry to miss it" in the context of a wedding into Spanish.

✦ Translate the phrase "Il faut cultiver notre jardin" into German.

✦ Translate the phrase "Happy birthday" into Japanese.

✦ Translate the phrase "Thank you for your hospitality" into French.

✦ Translate the phrase "Best wishes" in the context of a farewell party into Russian.

Explain Complex Topics

Prompt Formula

Provide a detailed comparison of the underlying themes of [idea A] and [idea B].

Prompt Examples

✦ Provide a detailed comparison of the underlying themes of quantum computing and classical computing.

✦ Provide a detailed comparison of the underlying themes of the political ideologies of conservatism and liberalism.

✦ Provide a detailed comparison of the underlying themes of the paintings *The Starry Night* by Vincent van Gogh and *The Persistence of Memory* by Salvador Dalí.

✦ Provide a detailed comparison of the underlying themes of Shakespeare's *Romeo and Juliet* and *Macbeth*.

✦ Provide a detailed comparison of the underlying themes of the economic theories of capitalism and socialism.

✦ Provide a detailed comparison of the underlying themes of the philosophies of existentialism and stoicism.

✦ Provide a detailed comparison of the underlying themes of the musical styles of jazz and classical music.

Discover Necessary Qualifications

Prompt Formula

In your opinion, what is the most important quality a [person] can possess in the context of [situation]?

Prompt Examples

✦ In your opinion, what is the most important quality a prompt engineer can possess, and why do you think that is?

✦ In your opinion, what is the most important quality a teacher can possess in the context of working with adults?

✦ In your opinion, what is the most important quality a parent can possess in the context of raising emotionally healthy children?

✦ In your opinion, what is the most important quality a leader can possess in the context of running a start-up?

✦ In your opinion, what is the most important quality a scientist can possess, and why do you think that is?

✦ In your opinion, what is the most important quality a friend can possess, and why do you think that is?

Discover Paths to Goals

Prompt Formula

Provide a list of [number] ways to [goal].

Prompt Examples

✦ Provide a list of 5 ways to be more productive in personal projects on weekends.

✦ Provide a list of 10 ways to adopt environmentally friendly habits with minimal effort.

✦ Provide a list of 8 ways to boost your confidence when interacting with your crush.

✦ Provide a list of 7 ways to improve your communication skills in professional settings.

✦ Provide a list of 6 ways to maintain a healthy work-life balance while working remotely.

✦ Provide a list of 9 ways to enhance your creativity during brainstorming sessions.

✦ Provide a list of 4 ways to effectively manage stress during high-pressure situations.

Get Concise Answers

Prompt Formula

Answer the following question in exactly [number] words: [question]?

Prompt Examples

✦ Answer the following question in exactly 10 words: How can I effectively manage my time during work?

✦ Answer the following question in exactly 20 words: What are some ways to reduce stress for a young adult?

✦ Answer the following question in exactly 5 words: What are some strategies for improving communication skills in my workplace?

✦ Answer the following question in exactly 6 words: What are some methods for increasing productivity when at home by myself?

✦ Answer the following question in exactly 8 words: What are the benefits of regular physical exercise?

✦ Answer the following question in exactly 12 words: How can I develop better decision-making skills in my career?

Analyze Popularity

Prompt Formula

What makes [title] such an [adjective] [media format]?

Prompt Examples

✦ What makes *Pulp Fiction* such a popular film?

✦ What makes *The Office* such a widely loved TV show?

✦ What makes Minecraft such an engaging video game?

✦ What makes Star Wars such an enduring movie franchise?

✦ What makes *The Great Gatsby* such a timeless novel?

✦ What makes the *Mona Lisa* such a captivating painting?

✦ What makes *Hamilton* such a groundbreaking musical?

✦ What makes the iPhone such an influential piece of technology?

Uncover Facts

Prompt Formula

What is an aspect of [subject] that is commonly misunderstood or overlooked by [group of people]?

Prompt Examples

+ What is an aspect of quantum mechanics that is commonly misunderstood by nonscientists?

+ What is an aspect of the history of the pencil that is commonly misunderstood or overlooked by students?

+ What is an aspect of the scientific properties of dreams that is commonly misunderstood or overlooked by adults?

+ What is an aspect of the cultural significance of blue that is commonly misunderstood or overlooked by designers?

+ What is an aspect of the history of jazz music that is commonly overlooked in mainstream narratives by musicians?

+ What is an aspect of the life and work of Vincent van Gogh that is commonly overlooked by art historians?

Learn a New Skill

Prompt Formula

Suggest practical ways to learn or practice [specific skill] without taking a course or joining a community.

Prompt Examples

✦ Suggest practical ways to learn or practice Python programming without taking a course or joining a community.

✦ Suggest practical ways to improve your public speaking skills without taking a course or joining a community.

✦ Suggest practical ways to learn basic financial management without taking a course or joining a community.

✦ Suggest practical ways to develop your leadership skills without taking a course or joining a community.

✦ Suggest practical ways to learn basic photography without taking a course or joining a community.

✦ Suggest practical ways to improve your time management skills without taking a course or joining a community.

✦ Suggest practical ways to improve your graphic design skills without taking a course or joining a community.

✦ Suggest practical ways to learn a new language without taking a course or joining a community.

Decorate Interiors

Prompt Formula

Come up with some interesting ways of decorating a [room/ space] in the style of [style]. The [element] should [goals].

Prompt Examples

✦ Come up with some interesting ways of decorating a bedroom in the style of a Harry Potter movie. The colors should match Gryffindor House.

✦ Come up with some interesting ways of decorating a living room in the style of mid-century modern. The furniture should emphasize clean lines and organic shapes.

✦ Come up with some interesting ways of decorating a bedroom in the style of bohemian. The color palette should feature rich, earthy tones and layers of texture.

✦ Come up with some interesting ways of decorating a home office in the style of industrial. The lighting should highlight exposed brick walls and metal accents.

✦ Come up with some interesting ways of decorating a kitchen in the style of a farmhouse. The cabinetry should showcase rustic wood finishes and vintage-inspired hardware.

✦ Come up with some interesting ways of decorating a garden space in the style of Japanese Zen. The water features should create a tranquil and meditative atmosphere.

✦ Come up with some interesting ways of decorating a dining room in the style of art deco. The wall art should incorporate bold geometric patterns and luxurious materials.

✦ Come up with some interesting ways of decorating a bathroom in the style of a coastal beach house. The accessories should evoke a relaxed, beachy vibe with soft colors and natural textures.

Analyze Content

Prompt Formula

Analyze this [format] for [purpose], such as [goals]: [insert text].

Prompt Examples

✦ Analyze this job application for professionalism, such as attention to detail, clear communication, and relevant experience: [insert job application].

✦ Analyze this poem for literary devices, such as imagery and metaphors: [insert text].

✦ Analyze this speech for persuasive techniques, such as ethos, pathos, and logos: [insert text].

✦ Analyze this marketing campaign for effectiveness, such as audience engagement, brand alignment, and call-to-action clarity: [insert PDF].

✦ Analyze this business proposal for feasibility, such as market demand and financial projections: [insert text].

✦ Analyze this user interface design for usability, such as navigation flow, accessibility compliance, and visual hierarchy: [insert image].

✦ Analyze this scientific study for methodology, such as experimental design and data analysis: [insert text].

✦ Analyze this website for user experience, such as navigation and visual design: [insert URL].

Learn How to Use Software

Prompt Formula

Using [software] and assuming a [skill level], outline the steps for [goal], including any necessary tips or resources.

Prompt Examples

✦ Using Photoshop and assuming an advanced skill level, outline the steps for removing the background of a picture, including any necessary tips or resources.

✦ Using WordPress and assuming a beginner skill level, outline the steps for creating a website, including any necessary tips or resources.

✦ Using Excel and assuming an intermediate skill level, outline the steps for creating a marketing budget, including any necessary tips or resources.

✦ Using Canva and assuming a beginner skill level, outline the steps for creating a social media post, including any necessary tips or resources.

✦ Using Adobe Premiere Pro and assuming an intermediate skill level, outline the steps for creating a video project, including any necessary tips or resources.

✦ Using Google Analytics and assuming a beginner skill level, outline the steps for setting up a website analytics dashboard, including any necessary tips or resources.

✦ Using Trello and assuming an intermediate skill level, outline the steps for managing a team project, including any necessary tips or resources.

✦ Using Unity and assuming an intermediate skill level, outline the steps for creating a 3D game environment, including any necessary tips or resources.

Discover Cultures

Prompt Formula

What are the most effective methods and resources for deepening my understanding of [place or group] culture, including strategies for engaging with the culture beyond the basics?

Prompt Examples

✦ What are the most effective methods and resources for deepening my understanding of European culture, including strategies for engaging with the culture beyond the basics?

✦ What are the most effective methods and resources for deepening my understanding of Japanese culture, including strategies for engaging with the culture beyond the basics?

✦ What are the most effective methods and resources for deepening my understanding of South American culture, including strategies for engaging with the culture beyond the basics?

✦ What are the most effective methods and resources for deepening my understanding of African culture, including strategies for engaging with the culture beyond the basics?

✦ What are the most effective methods and resources for deepening my understanding of Middle Eastern culture, including strategies for engaging with the culture beyond the basics?

✦ What are the most effective methods and resources for deepening my understanding of Indigenous cultures, including strategies for engaging with the culture beyond the basics?

✦ What are the most effective methods and resources for deepening my understanding of Asian culture, including strategies for engaging with the culture beyond the basics?

✦ What are the most effective methods and resources for deepening my understanding of LGBTQIA cultures, including strategies for engaging with the culture beyond the basics?

Create a Budget

Prompt Formula

Help me create a budget for my [monthly income] by allocating funds to [essential categories], [discretionary categories], and [savings/investments], while taking into account [financial goals].

Prompt Examples

✦ Help me create a budget for my $3,500 monthly income by allocating funds to rent, groceries, transportation, and health insurance (essential categories); concerts, weekend trips, and hobbies (discretionary categories); and debt repayment, emergency fund, and general savings (savings/investments), while taking into account saving for a wedding in 3 years.

✦ Help me create a budget for my $4,000 monthly income by allocating funds to rent, groceries, utilities, and insurance (essential categories); entertainment, dining out, and hobbies (discretionary categories); and retirement fund, emergency fund, and debt repayment (savings/investments), while taking into account purchasing a new car in 2 years.

✦ Help me create a budget for my $6,000 monthly income by allocating funds to mortgage, groceries, childcare, and transportation (essential categories); vacations, fitness memberships, and personal care (discretionary categories); and college fund, emergency fund, and retirement savings (savings/investments), while taking into account saving for a down payment on a home in 5 years.

✦ Help me create a budget for my $3,000 monthly income by allocating funds to rent, groceries, phone bill, and student loan payments (essential categories); movies, clothing, and gifts (discretionary categories); and retirement savings, emergency fund, and vacation savings (savings/investments), while taking into account paying off credit card debt in 12 months.

- Help me create a budget for my $4,500 monthly income by allocating funds to mortgage, groceries, utilities, and medical expenses (essential categories); home improvement, subscriptions, and dining out (discretionary categories); and emergency fund, retirement savings, and investment portfolio (savings/investments), while taking into account funding a sabbatical year for personal development.

- Help me create a budget for my $5,000 monthly income by allocating funds to mortgage, groceries, utilities, and childcare (essential categories); sports activities, personal development courses, and socializing (discretionary categories); and emergency fund, 401(k) contributions, and real estate investments (savings/investments), while taking into account a plan to retire early in 15 years.

Optimize Expenses

Prompt Formula

How can I optimize my [currency sum] monthly expenses while living in [location], in the categories of housing/utilities, transportation, and food by identifying cost-saving opportunities and implementing strategies such as negotiating, DIY, or comparison shopping?

Prompt Examples

✦ How can I optimize my $5,000 monthly expenses while living in New York City, in the categories of housing/utilities, transportation, and food by identifying cost-saving opportunities and implementing strategies such as negotiating, DIY, or comparison shopping?

✦ How can I optimize my €2,000 monthly expenses while living in the countryside of Germany, in the categories of housing/utilities, transportation, and food by identifying cost-saving opportunities and implementing strategies such as negotiating, DIY, or comparison shopping?

✦ How can I optimize my £9,000 monthly expenses while living in London, in the categories of housing/utilities, transportation, and food by identifying cost-saving opportunities and implementing strategies such as negotiating, DIY, or comparison shopping?

✦ How can I optimize my AUD 1,500 monthly expenses while living in Sydney, in the categories of housing/utilities, transportation, and food by identifying cost-saving opportunities and implementing strategies such as negotiating, DIY, or comparison shopping?

✦ How can I optimize my ARS 132.79 monthly expenses while living in Buenos Aires, in the categories of housing/utilities, transportation, and food by identifying cost-saving opportunities and implementing strategies such as negotiating, DIY, or comparison shopping?

✦ How can I optimize my $16,000 monthly expenses while living in San Francisco, in the categories of housing/utilities, transportation, and food by identifying cost-saving opportunities and implementing strategies such as negotiating, DIY, or comparison shopping?

✦ How can I optimize my €1,100 monthly expenses while living in Paris, in the categories of housing/utilities, transportation, and food by identifying cost-saving opportunities and implementing strategies such as negotiating, DIY, or comparison shopping?

Communicate Effectively

Prompt Formula

How can I effectively communicate my [beliefs] to others who are [characteristics], while understanding their [beliefs and perspectives]? What specific strategies can I use to promote understanding and respect for different viewpoints?

Prompt Examples

✦ How can I effectively communicate my human rights beliefs to others who have different cultural norms, while understanding their values and traditions? What specific strategies can I use to promote understanding and respect for different viewpoints?

✦ How can I effectively communicate my environmental beliefs to others who are skeptical about climate change, while understanding their concerns and perspectives? What specific strategies can I use to promote understanding and respect for different viewpoints?

✦ How can I effectively communicate my feminist beliefs to others who are resistant to gender equality, while understanding their values and cultural norms? What specific strategies can I use to promote understanding and respect for different viewpoints?

✦ How can I effectively communicate my artistic vision to others who are not familiar with contemporary art, while understanding their aesthetic preferences and interests? What specific strategies can I use to promote understanding and respect for different viewpoints?

✦ How can I effectively communicate my dietary beliefs to others who have different cultural or religious practices, while understanding their traditions and values? What specific strategies can I use to promote understanding and respect for different viewpoints?

✦ How can I effectively communicate my scientific beliefs to others who are skeptical of scientific evidence, while understanding their concerns and perspectives? What specific strategies can I use to promote understanding and respect for different viewpoints?

✦ How can I effectively communicate my spiritual beliefs to others who have different religious practices, while understanding their values and traditions? What specific strategies can I use to promote understanding and respect for different viewpoints?

Understand Others' Decisions

Prompt Formula

In [context/situation], what factors might influence someone to [action], and what are the potential consequences of this action?

Prompt Examples

✦ In a competitive job market, what factors might influence someone to pursue further education, and what are the potential consequences of this decision?

✦ In a pandemic, what factors might influence someone to get vaccinated, and what are the potential consequences of refusing to do so?

✦ In a romantic relationship, what factors might influence someone to forgive their partner after a betrayal, and what are the potential consequences of this forgiveness?

✦ In a high-pressure work environment, what factors might influence someone to take risks, and what are the potential consequences of this behavior?

✦ In a political campaign, what factors might influence someone to change their voting preferences, and what are the potential consequences of their decision?

✦ In a social media context, what factors might influence someone to share personal information online, and what are the potential consequences of this disclosure?

✦ In a sports competition, what factors might influence someone to cheat, and what are the potential consequences of this behavior?

✦ In a climate change context, what factors might influence someone to adopt eco-friendly habits, and what are the potential consequences of not doing so?

Teach Effectively

Prompt Formula

How can I effectively teach [person] to [activity], considering [challenges], and how can I evaluate their progress?

Prompt Examples

+ How can I effectively teach my grandmother to use a smartphone, considering her visual impairment and minimal previous technology experience, and how can I evaluate her progress?

+ How can I effectively teach my friend to play guitar, considering his extensive piano background and schedule constraints, and how can I evaluate his progress?

+ How can I effectively teach my colleague to give effective presentations, considering her timid communication style and fear of public speaking, and how can I evaluate her progress?

+ How can I effectively teach my coworker to use a new software program, considering her limited technical proficiency and time availability, and how can I evaluate her progress?

+ How can I effectively teach my partner to improve their language skills, considering their ambitious learning goals and international cultural background, and how can I evaluate their progress?

+ How can I effectively teach my child to swim by using flotation devices, considering their age and nonexistent swimming ability, and how can I evaluate their progress?

+ How can I effectively teach my employee to develop leadership skills, considering their ambitious career goals and personality traits, and how can I evaluate their progress?

Receive Relationship Advice

Prompt Formula

Act as a relationship coach. What would you recommend if I asked you for advice on the following issue: [relationship problem], taking into account the role and responsibility of each partner, the emotional and psychological impact of the problem, and the strategies for improving communication and trust?

Prompt Examples

✦ Act as a relationship coach. What would you recommend if I asked you for advice on the following issue: conflicts, taking into account the role and responsibility of each partner, the emotional and psychological impact of the problem, and the strategies for improving communication and trust?

✦ Act as a relationship coach. What would you recommend if I asked you for advice on the following issue: jealousy, taking into account the role and responsibility of each partner, the emotional and psychological impact of the problem, and the strategies for improving communication and trust?

✦ Act as a relationship coach. What would you recommend if I asked you for advice on the following issue: financial disagreements, taking into account the role and responsibility of each partner, the emotional and psychological impact of the problem, and the strategies for improving communication and trust?

✦ Act as a relationship coach. What would you recommend if I asked you for advice on the following issue: lack of intimacy, taking into account the role and responsibility of each partner, the emotional and psychological impact of the problem, and the strategies for improving communication and trust?

- Act as a relationship coach. What would you recommend if I asked you for advice on the following issue: differing parenting styles, taking into account the role and responsibility of each partner, the emotional and psychological impact of the problem, and the strategies for improving communication and trust?

- Act as a relationship coach. What would you recommend if I asked you for advice on the following issue: work-life balance, taking into account the role and responsibility of each partner, the emotional and psychological impact of the problem, and the strategies for improving communication and trust?

Overcome Fears

Prompt Formula

How can I overcome my fear of [activity] by identifying the root cause and triggers of the fear, considering the potential benefits and drawbacks of overcoming it?

Prompt Examples

✦ How can I overcome my fear of heights by identifying the root cause and triggers of the fear, considering the potential benefits and drawbacks of overcoming it?

✦ How can I overcome my fear of public speaking by identifying the root cause and triggers of the fear, considering the potential benefits and drawbacks of overcoming it?

✦ How can I overcome my fear of flying by identifying the root cause and triggers of the fear, considering the potential benefits and drawbacks of overcoming it?

✦ How can I overcome my fear of germs by identifying the root cause and triggers of the fear, considering the potential benefits and drawbacks of overcoming it?

✦ How can I overcome my fear of swimming by identifying the root cause and triggers of the fear, considering the potential benefits and drawbacks of overcoming it?

✦ How can I overcome my fear of social situations by identifying the root cause and triggers of the fear, considering the potential benefits and drawbacks of overcoming it?

✦ How can I overcome my fear of driving by identifying the root cause and triggers of the fear, considering the potential benefits and drawbacks of overcoming it?

✦ How can I overcome my fear of enclosed spaces (claustrophobia) by identifying the root cause and triggers of the fear, considering the potential benefits and drawbacks of overcoming it?

Balance Responsibilities

Prompt Formula

How can I effectively balance my [responsibilities] and make time for self-care?

Prompt Examples

✦ How can I effectively balance my busy work life and make time for self-care?

✦ How can I effectively balance my work responsibilities and make time for self-care?

✦ How can I effectively balance my family responsibilities and make time for self-care?

✦ How can I effectively balance my academic responsibilities and make time for self-care?

✦ How can I effectively balance my financial responsibilities and make time for self-care?

✦ How can I effectively balance my social responsibilities and make time for self-care?

✦ How can I effectively balance my community responsibilities and make time for self-care?

✦ How can I effectively balance my caregiving responsibilities and make time for self-care?

Snack Responsibly

Prompt Formula

Suggest some healthy and tasty snack options that are [flavor preference] and [dietary restriction] friendly.

Prompt Examples

✦ Suggest some healthy and tasty snack options that are sweet and low-carb friendly.

✦ Suggest some healthy and tasty snack options that are spicy and gluten-free.

✦ Suggest some healthy and tasty snack options that are garlic flavored and egg-free.

✦ Suggest some healthy and tasty citrus fruits that are keto-friendly.

✦ Suggest some healthy and tasty snack options that are chocolatey and vegan-friendly.

✦ Suggest some healthy and tasty snack options that are fruity and nut-free.

✦ Suggest some healthy and tasty snack options that are savory and dairy-free.

✦ Suggest some healthy and tasty snack options that are vegetables and paleo-friendly.

Discover Which Foods Can Improve Health

Prompt Formula

What are the best foods to eat for [health benefit], given a [restriction], and how can they be incorporated into [meal]?

Prompt Examples

✦ What are the best foods to eat for improving brain function, given a preference for spicy foods, and how can they be incorporated into lunch?

✦ What are the best anti-inflammatory foods to eat for joint pain, given a vegetarian diet, and how can they be incorporated into Indian cuisine?

✦ What are the best foods to eat for improving sleep, given a gluten intolerance, and how can they be incorporated into breakfast?

✦ What are the best foods to eat for improving heart health, given a preference for seafood, and how can they be incorporated into Mediterranean cuisine?

✦ What are the best foods to eat for reducing stress, given a low-carb diet, and how can they be incorporated into snack time?

✦ What are the best sources of iron for improving energy levels in women, and how can they be incorporated into plant-based meals?

✦ What are the best foods to eat for reducing inflammation, given a preference for Mexican cuisine, and how can they be incorporated into dinner?

✦ What are the best foods to eat for improving bone health, given a dairy intolerance, and how can they be incorporated into Asian cuisine?

Cook at Home

Prompt Formula

What are some options for [dish] that I can prepare/cook at home without any cooking experience, given [preference/restriction]?

Prompt Examples

✦ What are some options for comforting soups that I can prepare/cook at home without any cooking experience, given a preference for vegan meals?

✦ What are some options for easy-to-make smoothie bowls that I can prepare/cook at home without any cooking experience, given a dairy-free diet?

✦ What are some options for healthy snacks that I can prepare/cook at home without any cooking experience, given a nut allergy?

✦ What are some options for simple seafood dishes that I can prepare/cook at home without any cooking experience, given a desire to incorporate more omega-3s in my diet?

✦ What are some options for quick and easy plant-based dinners that I can prepare/cook at home without any cooking experience, given a busy schedule?

✦ What are some options for tasty and filling salads that I can prepare/cook at home without any cooking experience, given a desire to incorporate more vegetables in my diet?

✦ What are some options for gluten-free baked goods that I can prepare/cook at home without any cooking experience, given a wheat allergy?

✦ What are some options for meal prep lunches that I can prepare/cook at home without any cooking experience, given a goal to save time during the week?

Create a Workout Plan

Prompt Formula

Create a [workout] plan for a [height] [weight] [gender/age] with [fitness level] who wants to [specific goal] in [time period], incorporating [type of exercise].

Prompt Examples

✦ Create a strength training plan for a 6-foot, 170-pound male with intermediate experience who wants to increase their bench press weight by 10 pounds in a 3-month period, incorporating barbell exercises.

✦ Create a low-impact cardio plan for a 5-foot, 160-pound female with beginner-level fitness who wants to improve their cardiovascular endurance for a 5K race in 2 months, incorporating stationary biking and walking.

✦ Create a flexibility plan for a 5-foot, 110-pound 12-year-old child who wants to improve their splits in a 1-month period, incorporating stretching and yoga.

✦ Create a high-intensity interval training (HIIT) plan for a 6-foot, 200-pound male with advanced experience who wants to lose 15 pounds in a 4-month period, incorporating plyometric exercises and sprinting.

✦ Create a balance and stability plan for a 6-foot, 140-pound female with intermediate experience who wants to improve their surfing skills in a 2-month period, incorporating balance board exercises and yoga.

✦ Create a full-body workout plan for a 5-foot, 130-pound male with beginner-level fitness who wants to improve their overall strength and fitness in a 3-month period, incorporating bodyweight exercises and dumbbell workouts.

✦ Create a resistance band workout plan for a 5-foot, 100-pound 70-year-old female with intermediate experience who wants to improve their overall strength and flexibility in a 6-month period, incorporating resistance band exercises and stretching.

Create a Meal Plan

Prompt Formula

Create a [number]-day meal plan for an [age group] with [health condition/dietary preference/lifestyle habit] who needs to consume [number] calories per day, but make it [preference/restriction] to [goal].

Prompt Examples

✦ Create a 5-day meal plan for a 15-year-old with an aversion to dairy who needs to consume 2,000 calories per day, but make it dairy-free and calcium-rich to support bone health.

✦ Create a 14-day meal plan for a 40-year-old with a heavy workout schedule who needs to consume 1,800 calories per day, but make it low-carb and fiber-rich.

✦ Create a 30-day meal plan for a 60-year-old with hypertension who needs to consume 1,500 calories per day, but make it low-sodium and potassium-rich to manage blood pressure.

✦ Create a 21-day meal plan for a 25-year-old with a gluten allergy who needs to consume 2,500 calories per day, but make it high-fiber and iron-rich to support gut health and prevent nutrient deficiencies.

✦ Create a 7-day meal plan for a 35-year-old with polycystic ovary syndrome (PCOS) who needs to consume 2,000 calories per day, but make it low-glycemic and anti-inflammatory to manage hormonal imbalances and improve fertility.

✦ Create a 14-day meal plan for a 50-year-old trying to reduce snacking who needs to consume 1,800 calories per day, but make it veggie- and antioxidant-rich to support overall health.

Work Out at Home

Prompt Formula

What exercises can I do at home to improve my [body part] at a [experience level], incorporating [exercise]?

Prompt Examples

✦ What exercises can I do at home to improve my core and glutes at an intermediate level, incorporating planks and walking lunges?

✦ What exercises can I do at home to improve my cardiovascular endurance at a beginner level, incorporating jumping jacks and burpees?

✦ What exercises can I do at home to improve my shoulders at an intermediate level, incorporating resistance band pull-aparts and handstand push-ups?

✦ What exercises can I do at home to improve my power and explosiveness at an advanced level, incorporating Olympic lifts and plyometric jumps?

✦ What exercises can I do at home to improve my balance and stability at a beginner level, incorporating single-leg squats and yoga poses?

✦ What exercises can I do at home to improve my upper body strength at an advanced level, incorporating weighted pull-ups and dips?

✦ What exercises can I do at home to improve my flexibility at a beginner level, incorporating dynamic stretching and foam rolling?

✦ What exercises can I do at home to improve my speed and agility at an intermediate level, incorporating ladder drills and cone sprints?

Design Dinner Menus

Prompt Formula

Design a dinner menu with [number] courses, focusing on dishes that are [restriction] and cater to [food preferences].

Prompt Examples

✦ Design a dinner menu with 3 courses, focusing on dishes that are easy to cook for beginners and cater to vegetarian preferences.

✦ Design a dinner menu with 4 courses, focusing on dishes that require a preparation time of 30 minutes or less and cater to seafood lovers.

✦ Design a dinner menu with 2 courses, focusing on dishes that require no more than 6 ingredients and cater to vegan preferences.

✦ Design a dinner menu with 5 courses, focusing on dishes that require a preparation time of 20 minutes or less and cater to Asian cuisine preferences.

✦ Design a dinner menu with 3 courses, focusing on dishes that require no more than 7 ingredients and cater to Mexican cuisine preferences.

✦ Design a dinner menu with 4 courses, focusing on dishes that require a preparation time of 45 minutes or less and cater to Italian cuisine preferences.

✦ Design a dinner menu with 2 courses, focusing on dishes that require no more than 8 ingredients and cater to low-carb preferences.

✦ Design a dinner menu with 5 courses, focusing on dishes that require a preparation time of 60 minutes or less and cater to Mediterranean cuisine preferences.

Estimate the Future

Prompt Formula

How do you think [emerging technology] will impact the [industry] in the [short term/long term], and what are your expectations for this development?

Prompt Examples

+ How do you think autonomous vehicles will impact the transportation industry in the long term, and what are your expectations for this development?

+ How do you think artificial intelligence will impact the healthcare industry in the short term, and what are your expectations for this development?

+ How do you think virtual reality will impact the education industry in the long term, and what are your expectations for this development?

+ How do you think blockchain technology will impact investment banking within the finance industry in the short term, and what are your expectations for this development?

+ How do you think quantum computing will impact the cybersecurity industry in the short term, and what are your expectations for this development?

+ How do you think 3D printing will impact the manufacturing industry, specifically in aerospace, in the long term, and what are your expectations for this development?

+ How do you think the Internet of Things (IoT) will impact the smart city infrastructure in the short term, and what are your expectations for this development?

Explore Different Arguments

Prompt Formula

Write an argument [for/against] [subject] from multiple diverse perspectives. Before you do so, state the characteristics of the various characters.

Prompt Examples

✦ Write an argument for the use of artificial intelligence in universities from multiple diverse perspectives. Before you do so, state the characteristics of the various characters.

✦ Write an argument for universal basic income from multiple diverse perspectives. Before you do so, state the characteristics of the various characters.

✦ Write an argument against nuclear power from multiple diverse perspectives. Before you do so, state the characteristics of the various characters.

✦ Write an argument for veganism from multiple diverse perspectives. Before you do so, state the characteristics of the various characters.

✦ Write an argument against homeschooling from multiple diverse perspectives. Before you do so, state the characteristics of the various characters.

✦ Write an argument for the use of artificial intelligence in the job market from multiple diverse perspectives. Before you do so, state the characteristics of the various characters.

✦ Write an argument against the privatization of water resources from multiple diverse perspectives. Before you do so, state the characteristics of the various characters.

✦ Write an argument for space exploration from multiple diverse perspectives. Before you do so, state the characteristics of the various characters.

Generate Code for Randomization

Prompt Formula

Write [language] code that generates [desired output].

Prompt Examples

✦ Write PHP code that generates random business names.

✦ Write code in Ruby that generates a random haiku poem.

✦ Write code in Swift that generates a random workout routine with a specific number of exercises and sets.

✦ Write code in C# that generates a random math quiz with a specific number of questions and difficulty level.

✦ Write code in JavaScript that generates a random maze with a given size and complexity.

✦ Write code in Python that generates a random password of a specific length and complexity.

Create a Home Cleaning Schedule

Prompt Formula

Create a monthly cleaning schedule for a [type of home] fairly split across [number] people in the household.

Prompt Examples

✦ Create a monthly cleaning schedule for a 2-bedroom apartment fairly split across 2 people in the household.

✦ Create a monthly cleaning schedule for a 10-room colonial home fairly split across 5 people in the household.

✦ Create a monthly cleaning schedule for a 3-bedroom apartment fairly split across 6 roommates in the household.

✦ Create a monthly cleaning schedule for a small Cape home fairly split across 3 people in the household.

✦ Create a monthly cleaning schedule for a two-family home fairly split across 8 people in the household.

Research a Topic and Present Information in a Specific Way

Prompt Formula

Research [topic] and provide the results in [template/format].

Prompt Examples

✦ Research the top figures of early Greek democracy and provide the results in a list.

✦ Research frogs of the Amazon rainforest and provide the results in a list with names and photographs.

✦ Research the process of growing bananas and provide the results in a step-by-step format.

✦ Research the best Wi-Fi–enabled refrigerators on the market and provide the results in a table showing brand, model number, price, and reviews.

✦ Research the history of climate change and provide the results in a timeline.

✦ Research the most effective study techniques and provide the results in a list.

✦ Research the best pickup trucks and provide the results in a table showing car make, model, price, and reviews.

✦ Research often-overlooked nineteenth-century American poets and provide the results in a lesson format.

✦ Research the benefits of getting enough sleep and provide the results in a top 10 list.

✦ Research the most important moments in the history of spaceflight and provide the results in a timeline.

NOTES

Use the space here to add additional prompts that have worked well for you in this category.

CHAPTER 4

Personal Writing

Make Analogies

Prompt Formula

Create an analogy for [concept].

Prompt Examples

- Create an analogy for being overwhelmed.
- Create an analogy for explaining photosynthesis.
- Create an analogy for understanding how a computer processor works.
- Create an analogy for the concept of supply and demand in economics.
- Create an analogy for the process of cell division.
- Create an analogy for the theory of relativity.
- Create an analogy for the concept of machine learning.
- Create an analogy for the principle of buoyancy.

Write Anything

Prompt Formula

Using [writing style] and targeting [target audience], write a [type of text] for the [subject] in [location], highlighting the [key benefits] offered by the [subject].

Prompt Examples

✦ Using descriptive language and targeting luxury travelers, write a magazine article for a boutique hotel in Bali, highlighting the stunning views, serene atmosphere, and personalized service offered by the property.

✦ Using a casual writing style and targeting young adults, write a blog post for the new eco-friendly coffee shop in downtown Chicago, highlighting the sustainable practices and unique flavors offered by the coffee shop.

✦ Using a professional writing style and targeting business executives, write a press release for the upcoming tech conference in San Francisco, highlighting the networking opportunities and expert speakers offered by the event.

✦ Using a persuasive writing style and targeting parents of young children, write a brochure for the Montessori preschool in America, highlighting the child-centered approach and nurturing environment offered by the school.

✦ Using a narrative writing style and targeting adventure seekers, write a travel article for the hidden gem hiking trails in Colorado, highlighting the breathtaking views and challenging terrains offered by these trails.

✦ Using an informative writing style and targeting health-conscious individuals, write a newsletter for the recently launched organic grocery store Dallas, highlighting the wide variety of fresh produce and locally sourced products offered by the store.

- ✦ Using a descriptive writing style and targeting art enthusiasts, write an exhibition catalog for the contemporary art exhibit in Los Angeles, highlighting the innovative techniques and thought-provoking themes offered by the showcased artworks.

- ✦ Using a concise writing style and targeting busy professionals, write a product description for the latest time management app, highlighting the customizable features and productivity-boosting tools offered by the app.

Write Outlines

Prompt Formula

Provide an outline for [project].

Prompt Examples

✦ Provide an outline for a bachelor's thesis on solar power for rural areas.

✦ Provide an outline for a community garden project.

✦ Provide an outline for a software development project.

✦ Provide an outline for a school fundraising project.

✦ Provide an outline for a sustainable energy project.

✦ Provide an outline for a workplace diversity and inclusion project.

✦ Provide an outline for a mental health awareness campaign project.

✦ Provide an outline for a historical research project.

Write Profiles

Prompt Formula

Write a [type of profile] for [subject], highlighting their [description of interests/personality] in a way that is likely to attract [audience], using appropriate language and tone.

Prompt Examples

✦ Write a LinkedIn profile for Sarah, highlighting her expertise in project management and her collaborative and driven personality in a way that is likely to attract potential employers, using appropriate language and tone.

✦ Write a dating profile for John, highlighting his adventurous and free-spirited personality and interest in tennis in a way that is likely to attract like-minded individuals, using appropriate language and tone.

✦ Write a portfolio profile for a freelance graphic designer, highlighting their interest in digital art and attention to detail in a way that is likely to attract potential clients, using appropriate language and tone.

✦ Write a professional summary for a software developer, highlighting their technical skills in Python and C# and problem-solving ability in a way that is likely to attract potential employers, using appropriate language and tone.

✦ Write an artist bio for a painter, highlighting their minimalist artistic style and inspiration in a way that is likely to attract potential buyers and gallery owners, using appropriate language and tone.

✦ Write a personal statement for a graduate school application, highlighting the applicant's flawless SAT score and career aspirations in a way that is likely to attract admissions committees, using appropriate language and tone.

✦ Write an executive summary for a business plan, highlighting the unique value proposition focused on organic dog food that is locally sourced and market potential of the proposed product in a way that is likely to attract potential investors, using appropriate language and tone.

Write Speeches

Prompt Formula

Write a [type of speech] on a [specific topic].

Prompt Examples

✦ Write a TED talk about the power of mindfulness, exploring how it can lead to greater happiness and well-being.

✦ Write a commencement speech for a college graduation ceremony, discussing the importance of resilience and perseverance in navigating life's challenges.

✦ Write a wedding toast for my best friend's reception, sharing heartfelt anecdotes about our shared childhood in New Jersey and expressing love and appreciation for the newlyweds.

✦ Write a keynote speech for a technology conference, discussing the latest trends and innovations in artificial intelligence.

✦ Write a eulogy for a loved one's funeral, celebrating their life as a painter and their generousness and legacy.

✦ Write a campaign speech for a political candidate, outlining their optimistic vision for the city's downtown area and policies for the future.

✦ Write a motivational speech for a sports team, inspiring them to reach their full potential and achieve their goals.

✦ Write a farewell speech for a retiring colleague, expressing appreciation for their contributions to the HR department and wishing them well in their future endeavors.

Write Songs

Prompt Formula

Write a [type of song] about [subject], incorporating [additional details].

Prompt Examples

✦ Write a pop song about the challenges of growing up, incorporating elements of electronic dance music and using catchy hooks and relatable lyrics to capture the emotions and experiences of adolescence.

✦ Write a love ballad about my partner, incorporating elements of pop and R&B music and using metaphors and imagery to convey the depth of my emotions.

✦ Write a protest song about animal cruelty, incorporating elements of hip-hop and using powerful lyrics and a catchy chorus to rally support for the cause.

✦ Write a country song about my experiences growing up in a rural area, incorporating elements of bluegrass and using storytelling techniques and vivid descriptions to bring the setting to life.

✦ Write a rock song about the power of friendship, incorporating elements of punk and using driving guitar riffs and energetic lyrics to convey the intensity of the bond between friends.

✦ Write a jazz song about the beauty of nature, incorporating elements of swing and using improvisation and rich harmonies to capture the complexity and diversity of the natural world.

✦ Write a folk song about my family's Native American heritage, incorporating elements of Americana and using traditional instruments and vocal harmonies to convey the history and culture of my ancestors.

✦ Write a blues song about heartbreak and loss, incorporating elements of soul and using raw vocals and expressive guitar solos to convey the pain and sadness of the experience.

Write Stories

Prompt Formula

Act as a [type of storyteller]. Now write a [type of text] between [2 subjects].

Prompt Examples

✦ Act as a screenwriter. Now write a movie script between 2 astronauts stranded on a distant planet, using vivid descriptions and suspenseful plot developments to create a thrilling and visually stunning story.

✦ Act as a news reporter. Now write a news article between 2 political candidates discussing a controversial policy proposal, using objective reporting and journalistic techniques to present both sides of the argument.

✦ Act as a lyricist. Now write a song between 2 people falling in love, using poetic language and metaphorical imagery to capture the emotions and intensity of the relationship.

✦ Act as a mystery writer. Now write a detective story between 2 characters trying to solve a murder case, using plot twists and red herrings to keep the reader guessing until the very end.

✦ Act as a memoirist. Now write a personal essay between 2 family members discussing a difficult event from the past, using introspection and vivid details to convey the complexity of the relationship and the impact of the event.

✦ Act as a playwright. Now write a dialogue between 2 estranged friends trying to reconcile after a long period of separation, using dramatic tension and emotional conflict to create a powerful and memorable scene.

- ✦ Act as a historian. Now write a nonfiction book between 2 opposing sides of a war, using research and historical context to provide a comprehensive and balanced perspective on the conflict.

- ✦ Act as a humorist. Now write a comedy sketch between 2 characters dealing with an absurd situation, using witty dialogue and physical comedy to create a lighthearted and entertaining performance.

Write Social Media Captions

Prompt Formula

Come up with [adjective] captions for this [media] of [subject] for [target audience].

Prompt Examples

✦ Come up with engaging captions for this image of a subway car addressing the daily commute through New York City for commuters.

✦ Come up with humorous captions for this photo of a cat wearing sunglasses for cat lovers.

✦ Come up with inspirational captions for this video of a successful entrepreneur for aspiring business owners.

✦ Come up with educational captions for this infographic of the solar system for middle school students.

✦ Come up with romantic captions for this painting of a couple strolling by the beach for people celebrating anniversaries.

✦ Come up with witty captions for this meme of a famous movie scene for movie enthusiasts.

Write in a Specific Style

Prompt Formula

Write a [type of text] in the style of [author], covering [topic].

Prompt Examples

✦ Write a lecture in the style of Jordan B. Peterson, covering the importance of using headphones on a bus.

✦ Write a short story In the style of Ernest Hemingway, covering the theme of lost love.

✦ Write an article in the style of Hunter S. Thompson, covering the impact of social media on society.

✦ Write an essay in the style of George Orwell, covering the effects of surveillance on privacy.

✦ Write a screenplay in the style of Quentin Tarantino, covering the pursuit of justice in a crime-ridden city.

✦ Write a blog post in the style of David Foster Wallace, covering the impact of technology on human connection.

✦ Write a theater play in the style of Arthur Miller, covering the consequences of societal pressure on individuals.

Write Character Backgrounds

Prompt Formula

Write a character background story, using [style] to highlight their [characteristics] and [background].

Prompt Examples

✦ Write a character background story, using stream of consciousness to highlight their inner turmoil and traumatic experiences.

✦ Write a character background story, using magical realism to highlight their resilience and humble upbringing.

✦ Write a character background story, using film noir style to highlight their cunning nature and criminal past.

✦ Write a character background story, using Victorian Gothic style to highlight their secrecy and aristocratic lineage.

✦ Write a character background story, using allegory to highlight their leadership qualities and political struggles.

✦ Write a character background story, using dark humor to highlight their wit and complicated family dynamics.

Write Messages

Prompt Formula

Come up with a [type of text] for [type of company] that includes [type of reference].

Prompt Examples

✦ Come up with a press release for a machinery business that announces a merger.

✦ Come up with a press release for a tech company that includes quotes from industry experts.

✦ Come up with a press release for a nonprofit organization that includes stories from beneficiaries.

✦ Come up with a white paper for a financial institution that includes an analysis of industry trends.

Write Blog Posts

Prompt Formula

Come up with a [number]-word blog post for [type of website] that includes [specific references].

Prompt Examples

✦ Come up with a 200-word blog post for a health and wellness website that includes references to recent studies on the benefits of meditation, while also incorporating original content such as guided meditations or personal reflections on the practice.

✦ Come up with a 500-word blog post for a tech website that includes references to recent studies on the benefits of artificial intelligence, while also incorporating tips for prompting effectively.

✦ Come up with a 1,500-word blog post for a travel website that includes tips on how to travel to Paris, where to stay, and the top sites to visit.

✦ Come up with a 300-word blog post for a real estate website that includes tips on how to buy your first home, including finance options and how to assess the property's location.

Write Emotional Text

Prompt Formula

Write a [literary form] that includes [elements] to convey [emotion] about [subject].

Prompt Examples

✦ Write a short story that includes a protagonist who is struggling with addiction, a character who offers them support, and a moment of clarity to convey a sense of hope about recovery.

✦ Write a descriptive essay that includes sensory details about a specific location, personal reflections on its significance, and an overarching theme to convey a sense of nostalgia about the past.

✦ Write a dialogue that includes 2 characters with conflicting viewpoints, an unexpected turn of events, and a moment of understanding to convey a sense of empathy about the complexity of social issues.

✦ Write a persuasive essay that includes statistics on a current event, personal anecdotes, and a call to action to convey a sense of urgency about the need for social change.

✦ Write a poem that includes vivid imagery, a specific structure, and a recurring motif to convey a sense of longing about a lost love.

✦ Write a screenplay that includes a clear protagonist, a compelling antagonist, and a dramatic climax to convey a sense of catharsis about overcoming personal obstacles.

✦ Write a memoir that includes childhood memories, personal challenges, and reflections on growth to convey a sense of gratitude about life's journey.

✦ Write a research paper that includes an original thesis, compelling evidence, and a call to action to convey a sense of curiosity about a specific topic.

Write Video Scripts

Prompt Formula

Write a video script that [goal], exploring the topic of [subject] [additional details].

Prompt Examples

✦ Write a video script that outlines artificial intelligence, exploring the topic of its use in the creative industry.

✦ Write a video script that educates viewers on climate change, exploring the topic of greenhouse gases and their impact on global temperatures.

✦ Write a video script that entertains and informs, exploring the topic of ancient Egyptian culture and the construction of the Great Pyramid of Giza.

✦ Write a video script that motivates people to adopt a healthier lifestyle, exploring the topic of exercise and its benefits on mental and physical health.

✦ Write a video script that raises awareness about ocean pollution, exploring the topic of plastic waste and its effects on marine life.

✦ Write a video script that demystifies artificial intelligence, exploring the topic of machine learning and its applications in various industries.

✦ Write a video script that encourages viewers to practice mindfulness, exploring the topic of meditation and its positive effects on stress reduction.

✦ Write a video script that celebrates diversity, exploring the topic of cultural exchange and the importance of embracing different perspectives in a global society.

Write Artistic Performances

Prompt Formula

Create a [type of performance] that [subject], incorporating [additional details], to [goal].

Prompt Examples

✦ Create a stand-up comedy routine that highlights the absurdity of modern dating, incorporating witty observations and clever one-liners, to entertain and engage the audience.

✦ Create a spoken word performance that explores the experience of mental illness, incorporating personal reflections and social commentary, to raise awareness and promote empathy.

✦ Create a theatrical performance that depicts a historical event, incorporating immersive staging and period-specific costumes, to educate and entertain the audience.

✦ Create a dance performance that celebrates the diversity of human cultures, incorporating traditional movements and contemporary choreography, to promote cultural awareness and understanding.

✦ Create a musical performance that tells a story of overcoming adversity, incorporating powerful vocals and emotional lyrics, to inspire and uplift the audience.

✦ Create a magic performance that challenges conventional perceptions of reality, incorporating sleight of hand and mind-bending illusions, to entertain and amaze the audience.

✦ Create a circus performance that showcases the skills of a variety of performers, incorporating aerial acrobatics and daring stunts, to thrill and entertain the audience.

✦ Create a performance art piece that critiques consumerism and materialism, incorporating found objects and avant-garde techniques, to provoke thought and stimulate conversation.

Rewrite Carefully

Prompt Formula

Make the following text [desired outcome], without sacrificing [attribute or style]: [your text].

Prompt Examples

✦ Make the following text more engaging, without adding unnecessary fluff: [insert text].

✦ Make the following text more persuasive, without sounding pushy: [insert text].

✦ Make the following text more engaging, without sacrificing its professional tone: [insert text].

✦ Make the following text more approachable, without sacrificing its authoritative tone: [insert text].

✦ Make the following text more informative, without sacrificing its concise nature: [insert text].

✦ Make the following text more impactful: [insert text].

✦ Make the following text more inclusive: [insert text].

Rewrite Text in a Certain Tone

Prompt Formula

Rephrase the following text in a [specific style]: [insert text].

Prompt Examples

✦ Rephrase the following text in a more humorous style: [insert text].

✦ Rephrase the following text in a more formal style: [insert text].

✦ Rephrase the following text in a more persuasive style: [insert text].

✦ Rephrase the following text in a less casual style: [insert text].

✦ Rephrase the following text in a more casual style: [insert text].

Improve Existing Text

Prompt Formula

Improve this text by adding [elements] to [goal]: [insert text].

Prompt Examples

✦ Improve this text by adding comparisons to make the ideas more accessible and relatable for the reader: [insert text].

✦ Improve this text by adding sensory details and imagery to create a more vivid and immersive experience for the reader: [insert text].

✦ Improve this text by adding examples and statistics to support the arguments and make them more persuasive: [insert text].

✦ Improve this text by adding anecdotes and dialogue to make it more engaging and interactive for the reader: [insert text].

✦ Improve this text by adding descriptive language to create a more atmospheric setting: [insert text].

✦ Improve this text by adding emotional language to elicit an emotional response from the reader: [insert text].

✦ Improve this text by adding humor to make it more entertaining and engaging for the reader: [insert text].

Rewrite Persuasively

Prompt Formula

Evaluate whether this [point/object] is convincing and identify areas of improvement to make it [desired outcomes]. What specific changes can you make to achieve this goal: [goal]?

Prompt Examples

✦ Evaluate whether this point about education reform is convincing and identify areas of improvement to make it more practical, innovative, or well-supported. What specific changes can you make to achieve this goal: [goal]?

✦ Evaluate whether this argument in favor of renewable energy is convincing and identify areas of improvement to make it more persuasive, informative, or urgent. What specific changes can you make to achieve this goal: [goal]?

✦ Evaluate whether this argument in favor of increasing the minimum wage is convincing and identify areas of improvement to make it more compelling, fair, or urgent. What specific changes can you make to achieve this goal: [goal]?

✦ Evaluate whether this argument against genetically modified crops is convincing and identify areas of improvement to make it more professional, well-researched, or persuasive. What specific changes can you make to achieve this goal: [goal]?

✦ Evaluate whether this point about climate change is convincing and identify areas of improvement to make it more urgent, practical, or well-supported. What specific changes can you make to achieve this goal: [goal]?

✦ Evaluate whether this argument against animal testing is convincing and identify areas of improvement to make it more ethical, informative, or compelling. What specific changes can you make to achieve this goal: [goal]?

✦ Evaluate whether this argument in favor of a no-dogs-at-work policy is convincing and identify areas of improvement to make it more feasible, just, or evidence-based. What specific changes can you make to achieve this goal: [goal]?

Clarify Text Arguments

Prompt Formula

How can I clarify this argument about [argument] and identify potential areas that may be unclear or confusing to my audience? Make specific changes to achieve this goal: [goal].

Prompt Examples

✦ How can I clarify this argument about the benefits of implementing a work-from-home policy for employees and identify potential areas that may be unclear or confusing to my audience? Make specific changes to achieve this goal: [goal].

✦ How can I clarify this argument about the benefits of implementing a recycling program in our workplace and identify potential areas that may be unclear or confusing to my audience? Make specific changes to achieve this goal: [goal].

✦ How can I clarify this argument about the impact of climate change on coastal communities and identify potential areas that may be unclear or confusing to my audience? Make specific changes to achieve this goal: [goal].

✦ How can I clarify this argument about the benefits of implementing a new healthcare policy and identify potential areas that may be unclear or confusing to my audience? Make specific changes to achieve this goal: [goal].

✦ How can I clarify this argument about the effectiveness of a particular marketing strategy and identify potential areas that may be unclear or confusing to my audience? Make specific changes to achieve this goal: [goal].

✦ How can I clarify this argument about the role of technology in education and identify potential areas that may be unclear or confusing to my audience? Make specific changes to achieve this goal: [goal].

✦ How can I clarify this argument about the importance of mental health in the workplace and identify potential areas that may be unclear or confusing to my audience? Make specific changes to achieve this goal: [goal].

Write Heroic Stories

Prompt Formula

Craft a [genre] story about a protagonist who faces [conflict], resolves it through [resolution method], and experiences [character development], set in a [setting].

Prompt Examples

✦ Craft a fantasy story about a protagonist who faces the challenge of saving their kingdom from a great evil, resolves it through learning powerful magic, and experiences a loss of innocence, set in a mystical land.

✦ Craft a romance story about a protagonist who faces the challenge of long-distance love, resolves it through persistent communication, and experiences personal growth, set in a quaint coastal town.

✦ Craft a mystery story about a protagonist who faces the challenge of solving a murder, resolves it through keen observation, and experiences a newfound appreciation for life, set in a bustling city.

✦ Craft a coming-of-age story about a protagonist who faces the challenge of fitting in at a new school, resolves it through discovering their passion for music, and experiences self-discovery, set in a suburban neighborhood.

✦ Craft a thriller story about a protagonist who faces the challenge of escaping a hostage situation, resolves it through cunning manipulation, and experiences a new sense of bravery, set in a deserted office building.

✦ Craft a historical fiction story about a protagonist who faces the challenge of surviving through the American Civil War, resolves it through forging unlikely alliances, and experiences a deep sense of empathy, set in a small rural town.

✦ Craft a science fiction story about a protagonist who faces the challenge of finding a way to save Earth from an alien invasion, resolves it through discovering a powerful weapon, and experiences a new appreciation for the fragility of life, set in a futuristic city.

Invent Characters

Prompt Formula

Design a [character type] with a [backstory], [personality trait], [goal], [strength], and [weakness], who faces a [challenge] in a [story location] setting.

Prompt Examples

✦ Design a chef with a family legacy, a perfectionist personality, a goal of winning a culinary competition, a strength in creativity, and a weakness for anger management, who faces a rival chef in a high-pressure kitchen setting.

✦ Design a detective with a tragic past, a sharp eye for detail, a goal of solving a high-profile case, a strength in deduction, and a weakness for substance abuse, who faces a serial killer in a gritty urban setting.

✦ Design a witch with a mysterious ancestry, a mischievous streak, a goal of mastering a powerful spell, a strength in potion-making, and a weakness for forbidden magic, who faces a coven of rival witches in a magical forest setting.

✦ Design a soldier with a heroic background, a no-nonsense attitude, a goal of protecting their squad, a strength in combat, and a PTSD weakness, who faces an enemy ambush in a war zone setting.

✦ Design a musician with a troubled childhood, a melancholic temperament, a goal of composing a hit song, a strength in playing multiple instruments, and a weakness for stage fright, who faces a critical music reviewer in a music festival setting.

✦ Design a scholar with a curiosity for the unknown, a reserved personality, a goal of deciphering an ancient script, a strength in historical research, and a weakness for social skills, who faces a hidden organization in a remote archaeological site setting.

✦ Design a con artist with a checkered past, a charming personality, a goal of pulling off a heist, a strength in deception, and a weakness for greed, who faces a ruthless crime boss in a casino setting.

Write Interviews

Prompt Formula

Compose a [format] interview with [type of professional] discussing their experience with [topic], including [number] insightful questions and exploring [specific aspect].

Prompt Examples

+ Compose a video interview with a software engineer discussing their experience with artificial intelligence, including 12 insightful questions and exploring the ethical implications of AI.

+ Compose a magazine interview with a fashion designer discussing their experience with sustainable fashion, including 8 insightful questions and exploring their latest eco-friendly collection.

+ Compose a podcast interview with a nutritionist discussing their experience with plant-based diets, including 10 insightful questions and exploring the benefits and challenges of such a diet.

+ Compose a radio interview with a historian discussing their experience with ancient civilizations, including 6 insightful questions and exploring their latest research on a specific civilization.

+ Compose a blog interview with a sports coach discussing their experience with building team culture, including 8 insightful questions and exploring their coaching philosophy.

+ Compose a webinar interview with a mental health professional discussing their experience with mindfulness techniques, including 10 insightful questions and exploring the benefits of mindfulness for mental health.

+ Compose a newspaper interview with an entrepreneur discussing their experience with starting a successful business, including 5 insightful questions and exploring the challenges and opportunities of entrepreneurship.

Practice Writing

Prompt Formula

Develop a [writing technique] exercise for [skill level] writers that involves [specific task], with a focus on improving [aspect of writing].

Prompt Examples

✦ Develop a plot development exercise for intermediate-level writers that involves creating a story outline, with a focus on improving story structure and pacing.

✦ Develop a dialogue exercise for beginner-level writers that involves writing a conversation between two characters, with a focus on improving natural-sounding dialogue.

✦ Develop a worldbuilding exercise for advanced-level writers that involves creating a detailed setting description, with a focus on improving sensory details and world consistency.

✦ Develop a sensory writing exercise for beginner-level writers that involves writing a paragraph description of a setting, with a focus on improving sensory detail usage.

✦ Develop a character dialogue exercise for intermediate-level writers that involves writing a conversation between two characters with opposing viewpoints, with a focus on improving conflict and tension.

✦ Develop an editing exercise for advanced-level writers that involves rewriting a paragraph for clarity and concision, with a focus on improving precision and flow.

✦ Develop a poetry exercise for beginner-level writers that involves writing a free verse poem, with a focus on improving imagery and figurative language usage.

Create Worlds

Prompt Formula

Design a [type of world] for a [genre] story, including its [geographical features], [societal structure], [culture], and key historical events that influence the plot/characters.

Prompt Examples

✦ Design a cyberpunk world for a dystopian sci-fi story, including its urban landscape, social hierarchy, counterculture, and key historical events that influence the plot/characters.

✦ Design an underwater world for a deep-sea fantasy story, including its bioluminescent cities, aquatic civilizations, mysterious krakens, and key oceanic cataclysms that influence the plot/characters.

✦ Design a post-apocalyptic world for a survival horror story, including its harsh environments, warring factions, mutated creatures, and key historical events that influence the plot/characters.

✦ Design a historical world for a historical fiction story, including its political landscape, social norms, cultural practices, and key historical events that influence the plot/characters.

✦ Design a magical world for a young adult fantasy story, including its enchanted forests, magical creatures, wizarding schools, and key historical events that influence the plot/characters.

✦ Design a space opera world for a space adventure story, including its planetary systems, intergalactic civilizations, alien species, and key historical events that influence the plot/characters.

✦ Design a supernatural world for a paranormal romance story, including its paranormal creatures, supernatural powers, forbidden romances, and key historical events that influence the plot/characters.

Write Character Arcs

Prompt Formula

Design a [type of character arc] for a [protagonist] in a [genre] story, detailing their [starting point], [growth], [struggle], and [resolution].

Prompt Examples

✦ Design a redemption arc for a detective in a noir mystery story, detailing their cynical worldview, moral awakening, ethical dilemma, and sacrificial redemption.

✦ Design a coming-of-age arc for a teenager in a young adult romance story, detailing their naiveté, self-discovery, heart-break, and self-acceptance.

✦ Design a hero's journey arc for a warrior in an epic fantasy story, detailing their call to adventure, mentorship, trials, and ultimate victory against evil.

✦ Design a survivor's guilt arc for a soldier in a war drama story, detailing their patriotic duty, traumatic experiences, survivor's guilt, and eventual healing through helping others.

✦ Design a midlife crisis arc for a housewife in a domestic fiction story, detailing their suburban ennui, rebellious phase, existential crisis, and renewed purpose through community service.

✦ Design a rags-to-riches arc for an entrepreneur in a business novel, detailing their humble beginnings, strategic innovation, ethical challenges, and philanthropic legacy.

✦ Design a self-destruction arc for a celebrity in a Hollywood satire, detailing their narcissistic excess, public scandals, personal downfall, and eventual comeback with humility.

Write Dialogues

Prompt Formula

Craft a [type of dialogue] between [number] characters with [distinct situations] discussing [topic] in a [setting] and ending with an [outcome].

Prompt Examples

+ Craft a suspenseful negotiation between 3 spies with hidden agendas discussing a sensitive mission in a dark alley and ending with a betrayal.

+ Craft a heated argument between 2 siblings with contrasting personalities discussing their parents' estate in a lawyer's office and ending with a compromise.

+ Craft a friendly banter between 3 colleagues with diverse backgrounds discussing their favorite TV shows in a coffee shop and ending with a consensus.

+ Craft a philosophical debate between 4 scholars with different perspectives discussing the meaning of life in a university seminar room and ending with a deadlock.

+ Craft a flirtatious conversation between 2 strangers with magnetic chemistry discussing their dreams and fears on a park bench and ending with a date.

+ Craft a humorous gossip session between 4 women with juicy secrets discussing a scandalous rumor in a beauty salon and ending with a revelation.

+ Craft a poignant confession between 2 lovers with unresolved conflicts discussing their past mistakes in a candlelit bedroom and ending with a reconciliation.

Use the space here to add additional prompts that
have worked well for you in this category.

CHAPTER 5

Creativity & Fun

Find the Perfect Gift

Prompt Formula

I need help finding the perfect gift. The gift is for [person] and they are interested in [interests]. It's a gift for [occasion] and my budget is [range]. Using this information, please search and compile a list of 3–5 unique and thoughtful gift ideas, along with a short explanation for why each one might be a great fit.

Prompt Examples

✦ I need help finding the perfect gift. The gift is for my father, and he is interested in gardening, jogging, and World War II history. It's a gift for Father's Day and my budget is $50–$75. Using this information, please search and compile a list of 3–5 unique and thoughtful gift ideas, along with a short explanation for why each one might be a great fit.

✦ I need help finding the perfect gift. The gift is for my coworker and they are interested in running, listening to vinyl music, and craft beer. It's a gift for their birthday and my budget is $30. Using this information, please search and compile a list of 3–5 unique and thoughtful gift ideas, along with a short explanation for why each one might be a great fit.

✦ I need help finding the perfect gift. The gift is for my sister and she is interested in jewelry, dogs, and the Los Angeles Dodgers. It's a gift for her college graduation and my budget is $100. Using this information, please search and compile a list of 3–5 unique and thoughtful gift ideas, along with a short explanation for why each one might be a great fit.

✦ I need help finding the perfect gift. The gift is for my child's teacher and they are interested in books, reality TV, and crossword puzzles. It's a gift for the end of the school year and my budget is $50. Using this information, please search and compile a list of 3–5 unique and thoughtful gift ideas, along with a short explanation for why each one might be a great fit.

Discover Funny Nicknames

Prompt Formula

Come up with [number] funny nicknames for [subject] that incorporate a play on words.

Prompt Examples

✦ Come up with 5 funny nicknames for a dog that incorporate a play on words.

✦ Come up with 3 funny nicknames for a mathematician that incorporate a play on words.

✦ Come up with 5 funny nicknames for a chef that incorporate a play on words.

✦ Come up with 4 funny nicknames for a musician that incorporate a play on words.

✦ Come up with 6 funny nicknames for a programmer that incorporate a play on words.

✦ Come up with 7 funny nicknames for a gardener that incorporate a play on words.

✦ Come up with 2 funny nicknames for a dentist that incorporate a play on words.

Exaggerate Anything

Prompt Formula

Exaggerate the following statement to [goal]: [statement].

Prompt Examples

✦ Exaggerate the following statement sheets to motivate someone to exercise: I should go to the gym.

✦ Exaggerate the following statement to convince someone to take action: I should eat healthier.

✦ Exaggerate the following statement to entertain a child: The sun is hot.

✦ Exaggerate the following statement to express frustration: I can't find my keys.

✦ Exaggerate the following statement based on the following statement: I need a vacation.

✦ Exaggerate the following statement to scare someone: Spiders are harmless.

✦ Exaggerate the following statement to express gratitude: I appreciate your help.

✦ Exaggerate the following statement based on the following statement: I want to be successful.

Create an ASCII Image

Prompt Formula

Create an ASCII art image showing [subject].

Prompt Examples

✦ Create an ASCII art image showing a dragon breathing fire.

✦ Create an ASCII art image showing a starry night sky.

✦ Create an ASCII art image showing a clownfish swimming.

✦ Create an ASCII art image showing a complex maze.

✦ Create an ASCII art image showing a city skyline.

✦ Create an ASCII art image showing a haunted house that conveys a sense of foreboding.

✦ Create an ASCII art image showing a panda eating bamboo.

✦ Create an ASCII art image showing a beach scene with palm trees and a sunset.

Write Ridiculous Stories

Prompt Formula

Write a [type of story] about a [subject] [action] [goal].

Prompt Examples

✦ Write a fable about a frog that learns to fly and becomes the king of the birds.

✦ Write a science fiction story about a cactus that learns to communicate with aliens and saves the world.

✦ Write a romantic comedy about a robot that learns to love and wins the heart of a human.

✦ Write a spy thriller about a hamster that becomes a double agent for rival pet stores.

✦ Write a western about a cow that learns to play poker and wins a high-stakes game.

✦ Write a dystopian story about a butterfly that gains the ability to think and rebels against their oppressive society.

✦ Write a children's book about a penguin that learns to surf and saves their ocean community from pollution.

Write Jokes

Prompt Formula

Provide a [type, if desired] joke about [subject].

Prompt Examples

✦ Provide a joke about a zombie that has lost all of its limbs.

✦ Provide a one-liner joke about a tomato.

✦ Provide a knock-knock joke about a mushroom.

✦ Provide a joke about a lawyer in a courtroom setting.

✦ Provide a joke about a mathematician.

✦ Provide a joke about a ghost in a haunted house.

✦ Provide a joke about a scientist.

✦ Provide a joke about a politician.

✦ Provide a joke about a musician.

Discover Pickup Lines

Prompt Formula

Formulate pickup lines as if [unusual style].

Prompt Examples

✦ Formulate pickup lines as if you were a chef trying to impress someone with your culinary skills.

✦ Formulate pickup lines as if you were a robot programmed to flirt.

✦ Formulate pickup lines as if you were a time traveler trying to woo someone from the past.

✦ Formulate pickup lines as if you were a romantic vampire.

✦ Formulate pickup lines as if you were a famous literary character.

✦ Formulate pickup lines as if you were a street performer.

✦ Formulate pickup lines as if you were a detective trying to solve a romantic mystery.

✦ Formulate pickup lines as if you were a comedian trying to win over a tough crowd.

Discover Puns

Prompt Formula

Provide a list of puns related to [subject].

Prompt Examples

+ Provide a list of puns related to fashion.
+ Provide a list of puns related to cooking.
+ Provide a list of puns related to sports.
+ Provide a list of puns related to holidays.
+ Provide a list of puns related to psychology.
+ Provide a list of puns related to weather.
+ Provide a list of puns related to technology.
+ Provide a list of puns related to music.

Discover Wordplays

Prompt Formula

Create a wordplay on [subject] that makes me laugh.

Prompt Examples

✦ Create a wordplay on Instagram models that makes me laugh.

✦ Create a wordplay on vegetables that makes me laugh.

✦ Create a wordplay on video games that makes me laugh.

✦ Create a wordplay on the ocean that makes me laugh.

✦ Create a wordplay on time that makes me laugh.

✦ Create a wordplay on the human body that makes me laugh.

✦ Create a wordplay on pets that makes me laugh.

✦ Create a wordplay on technology that makes me laugh.

Discover Ridiculous Questions

Prompt Formula

Come up with a list of ridiculous hypothetical questions about [subject].

Prompt Examples

✦ Come up with a list of ridiculous hypothetical questions about marriage.

✦ Come up with a list of ridiculous hypothetical questions about monsters.

✦ Come up with a list of ridiculous hypothetical questions about time travel.

✦ Come up with a list of ridiculous hypothetical questions about sports.

✦ Come up with a list of ridiculous hypothetical questions about technology.

✦ Come up with a list of ridiculous hypothetical questions about the human body.

✦ Come up with a list of ridiculous hypothetical questions about space exploration.

✦ Come up with a list of ridiculous hypothetical questions about education.

Discover Clever Excuses

Prompt Formula

Act as if you are a [character] and come up with a clever excuse for why you can't do [task].

Prompt Examples

✦ Act as if you are a surfer bro and come up with a clever excuse for why you can't get a job.

✦ Act as if you are a pirate and come up with a clever excuse for why you can't sail the ship.

✦ Act as if you are a movie star and come up with a clever excuse for why you can't act in the movie.

✦ Act as if you are a chef and come up with a clever excuse for why you can't cook the meal.

✦ Act as if you are a superhero and come up with a clever excuse for why you can't save the city.

✦ Act as if you are a poet and come up with a clever excuse for why you can't write a sonnet.

Write Funny Excuses

Prompt Formula

Write a lengthy excuse for not attending [event] in the style of [author], using their [special skills] to craft a compelling and humorous excuse.

Prompt Examples

✦ Write a lengthy excuse for not attending a friend's wedding in the style of Charles Dickens, using their vivid descriptions and characterizations to craft a compelling and humorous excuse.

✦ Write a lengthy excuse for not attending a colleague's retirement party in the style of Mark Twain, using their humor and wit to craft a compelling and humorous excuse.

✦ Write a lengthy excuse for not attending a family reunion in the style of Jane Austen, using their formal language and social commentary to craft a compelling and humorous excuse.

✦ Write a lengthy excuse for not attending a company Christmas party in the style of Ernest Hemingway, using their concise and direct writing style to craft a compelling and humorous excuse.

✦ Write a lengthy excuse for not attending a friend's baby shower in the style of Virginia Woolf, using their stream-of-consciousness narrative style and introspection to craft a compelling and humorous excuse.

✦ Write a lengthy excuse for not attending a book club meeting in the style of F. Scott Fitzgerald, using their poetic language and romanticism to craft a compelling and humorous excuse.

✦ Write a lengthy excuse for not attending a charity gala in the style of Emily Brontë, using their dark and passionate writing style to craft a compelling and humorous excuse.

✦ Write a lengthy excuse for not attending a birthday party in the style of William Shakespeare, using their poetic language and literary allusions to craft a compelling and humorous excuse.

Convert Text to Ridiculous Code

Prompt Formula

Convert the given text into the esoteric programming language Brainfuck: [text].

Prompt Examples

✦ Convert the given text into the esoteric programming language Brainfuck: Hello, world!

✦ Convert the given text into the esoteric programming language Brainfuck: Let there be light.

✦ Convert the given text into the esoteric programming language Brainfuck: I love coding.

✦ Convert the given text into the esoteric programming language Brainfuck: ChatGPT is awesome.

✦ Convert the given text into the esoteric programming language Brainfuck: The quick brown fox jumps over the lazy dog.

✦ Convert the given text into the esoteric programming language Brainfuck: To be or not to be.

✦ Convert the given text into the esoteric programming language Brainfuck: artificial intelligence.

✦ Convert the given text into the esoteric programming language Brainfuck: GPT-4 is powerful.

Discover New Movies

Prompt Formula

Create a table listing the top 10 [category] options to help you unwind after a long day. The first column is titled "Name", the second column is "Description", the third column is "Average Rating (Out of 5)", and the fourth column is "Top Critic Quote".

Prompt Examples

✦ Create a table listing the top 10 comedy movie options to help you unwind after a long day. The first column is titled "Name", the second column is "Description", the third column is "Average Rating (Out of 5)", and the fourth column is "Top Critic Quote".

✦ Create a table listing the top 10 sci-fi movie options to help you unwind after a long day. The first column is titled "Name", the second column is "Description", the third column is "Average Rating (Out of 5)", and the fourth column is "Top Critic Quote".

✦ Create a table listing the top 10 animated movie options to help you unwind after a long day. The first column is titled "Name", the second column is "Description", the third column is "Average Rating (Out of 5)", and the fourth column is "Top Critic Quote".

✦ Create a table listing the top 10 action movie options to help you unwind after a long day. The first column is titled "Name", the second column is "Description", the third column is "Average Rating (Out of 5)", and the fourth column is "Top Critic Quote".

✦ Create a table listing the top 10 thriller movie options to help you unwind after a long day. The first column is titled "Name", the second column is "Description", the third column is "Average Rating (Out of 5)", and the fourth column is "Top Critic Quote".

✦ Create a table listing the top 10 documentary movie options to help you unwind after a long day. The first column is titled "Name", the second column is "Description", the third column is "Average Rating (Out of 5)", and the fourth column is "Top Critic Quote".

✦ Create a table listing the top 10 fantasy movie options to help you unwind after a long day. The first column is titled "Name", the second column is "Description", the third column is "Average Rating (Out of 5)", and the fourth column is "Top Critic Quote".

✦ Create a table listing the top 10 foreign-language movie options to help you unwind after a long day. The first column is titled "Name", the second column is "Description", the third column is "Average Rating (Out of 5)", and the fourth column is "Top Critic Quote".

Talk to Historical Figures

Prompt Formula

Pretend you are [historical figure] explaining [topic] to me. Let's have a dialogue where I can ask questions to understand [topic].

Prompt Examples

✦ Pretend you are Winston Churchill explaining World War II to me. Let's have a dialogue where I can ask questions to understand post-war diplomacy.

✦ Pretend you are Martin Luther King Jr. explaining the civil rights movement to me. Let's have a dialogue where I can ask questions to understand nonviolent protest.

✦ Pretend you are Ada Lovelace explaining the origins of computer programming to me. Let's have a dialogue where I can ask questions to understand algorithms.

✦ Pretend you are Socrates explaining philosophy to me. Let's have a dialogue where I can ask questions to understand the Socratic method.

✦ Pretend you are Frida Kahlo explaining her self-portraits to me. Let's have a dialogue where I can ask questions to understand *The Two Fridas*.

✦ Pretend you are Albert Einstein explaining the theory of relativity to me. Let's have a dialogue where I can ask questions to understand time dilation.

Discover New Books

Prompt Formula

Create a table listing the top [number] [category] books that [describe specific focus]. The first column is titled "Title", the second column is "Author", the third column is "Description", the fourth column is "Average Rating (Out of 5)", and the fifth column is "Top Critic Quote".

Prompt Examples

✦ Create a table listing the top 10 sci-fi books that deal with life in outer space. The first column is titled "Title", the second column is "Author", the third column is "Description", the fourth column is "Average Rating (Out of 5)", and the fifth column is "Top Critic Quote".

✦ Create a table listing the top 5 children's books that focus on the first day of school. The first column is titled "Title", the second column is "Author", the third column is "Description", the fourth column is "Average Rating (Out of 5)", and the fifth column is "Top Critic Quote".

✦ Create a table listing the top 3 biographies that feature entrepreneurs. The first column is titled "Title", the second column is "Author", the third column is "Description", the fourth column is "Average Rating (Out of 5)", and the fifth column is "Top Critic Quote".

✦ Create a table listing the top 10 books that were made into award-winning movies. The first column is titled "Title", the second column is "Author", the third column is "Description", the fourth column is "Average Rating (Out of 5)", and the fifth column is "Top Critic Quote".

- ✦ Create a table listing the top 3 history books about American military strategy in World War II. The first column is titled "Title", the second column is "Author", the third column is "Description", the fourth column is "Average Rating (Out of 5)", and the fifth column is "Top Critic Quote".

- ✦ Create a table listing the top 5 romance books that feature a Black heroine. The first column is titled "Title", the second column is "Author", the third column is "Description", the fourth column is "Average Rating (Out of 5)", and the fifth column is "Top Critic Quote".

- ✦ Create a table listing the top 10 beach reads that are available in paperback. The first column is titled "Title", the second column is "Author", the third column is "Description", the fourth column is "Average Rating (Out of 5)", and the fifth column is "Top Critic Quote".

- ✦ Create a table listing the top 5 cookbooks that feature healthy Mediterranean cooking. The first column is titled "Title", the second column is "Author", the third column is "Description", the fourth column is "Average Rating (Out of 5)", and the fifth column is "Top Critic Quote".

NOTES

Use the space here to add additional prompts that have worked well for you in this category.

PART 3

Polishing Your Prompts

CHAPTER 6

Follow-Up Prompts

After you've submitted your initial prompt, you can turn to the options in this section for additional follow-up prompts. They can help you clarify, refine, and deepen your requests to get even closer to exactly what you need.

Universal Follow-Up Options

✦ **Try Again**
Could you elaborate on how the latest response you provided doesn't align with my previous instructions? After clarifying that, please make another attempt at following the instructions I gave earlier.

✦ **Clarify Concept**
Can you clarify what you mean by [concept]?

✦ **Multiply Input**
What would change if I invested 10 times more time or energy?

✦ **Summarize Conversation**
Write a summary of our conversation in bullet points.

✦ **Explore Details**
Now explain that in more detail.

✦ **Go Deeper**
But why?

✦ **Multiply Results**
Please supply 10 more.

Options for Transforming the Response

✦ **Change the Style**
Rewrite in the style of [style].

✦ **Add Context**
Now try again but consider [context].

✦ **Change Text Type**
Now transform all the above information into a [text type].

Options for Problem-Solving Based on the Response

✦ **Find Cheaper Solutions**

If we had to solve this problem with half the resources or time, what would we do differently?

✦ **Brainstorm Solutions**

What are some other ideas or solutions we haven't considered yet? Can you think of any creative ways to approach this problem?

Options for Analyzing
the Impact of a Decision

✦ **Measure Success**

What would success look like in this situation and how can we measure it? Format the answer in a table with two columns titled "Success Criteria" and "Measurement Method".

✦ **Estimate Impact**

How will this decision affect different stakeholders? Are there any potential conflicts of interest?

Options for Efficient Planning Follow-Up

✦ **Break Down Steps**

Break this down into smaller steps. Summarize them in a to-do list.

✦ **Explore Next Steps**

Summarize the main points we've discussed so far in a bullet point list. Based on our conversation, what would you recommend as the next steps?

✦ **Detailed Plan**

Outline a step-by-step plan for implementing this solution. What actions should we take first? Format the answer in a table with a column for steps and a second column for solutions.

Options to Help Further Analyze a Situation

✦ **Consider Feedback**

Do you have any feedback or suggestions on the current approach? How can we improve it? Provide real-world examples to illustrate your point.

✦ **Weigh Pros/Cons**

What are the advantages and disadvantages of this approach? How does this solution compare to others?

✦ **Find the Best Solution**

Why do you think that is the best solution? What factors led you to this conclusion?

Options That Focus On
Learning a Topic Quickly

✦ **Clarify Misconceptions**
What are some common misconceptions or misunderstandings about this topic that beginners should be aware of?

✦ **Simplify Learning**
Break this down into simpler terms or steps for someone who is new to the topic while making it understandable for a 5-year-old.

✦ **Get Tips/Advice**
What practical and immediately actionable tips or advice would you give to someone just starting out in this area?

✦ **Identify Key Skills**
What are the most important skills or knowledge areas for beginners to focus on in this field?

Options to Change the Tone of the Response

Run the prompt again, but this time customize your text by including the phrase "make the text [tone]." Here are some choices:

✦ **Formal Tone**
Projects authority, professionalism, and seriousness; often used in academic or official contexts.

✦ **Informal Tone**
Creates a casual, conversational atmosphere; suitable for relaxed or personal contexts.

✦ **Authoritative Tone**
Conveys expertise, decisiveness, and confidence; suitable for presenting expert opinions.

✦ **Conversational Tone**
Mimics the natural flow and rhythm of spoken language; creates an informal, relatable tone.

✦ **Empathetic Tone**
Demonstrates understanding, compassion, or sensitivity; connects with readers emotionally.

✦ **Educational Tone**
Demonstrates curiosity with an aim for clarity on a particular topic; suitable for learning new topics.

Options to Change the Style of the Response

Run the prompt again, but this time customize your text by including "in the style of [brand voice]." Here are some choices:

✦ **Rolling Stone Magazine**
Music, culture, and politics

✦ **Wired Magazine**
Technology, science, and culture

✦ **Vogue Magazine**
Fashion, beauty, and culture

✦ **The Wall Street Journal**
Business, finance, and politics

✦ **Aesthetica Magazine**
Art, culture, and photography

✦ **Nike**
Empowerment, athleticism, and motivation

✦ **Disney**
Magic, family entertainment, and storytelling

✦ **Harley-Davidson**
Freedom, individualism, and the American spirit

✦ **Rolex**
Precision, craftsmanship, and prestige

✦ **Vans**
Authenticity, youth culture, and action sports

What's Next?

Look where you are now.

You started with a simple joke about your favorite animal. Now you're crafting prompts, teaching AI your writing style, and creating content that actually sounds like you. You didn't just read about it; you actually did it. That hands-on practice is what separates you from everyone else who's still just talking about AI.

Your Digital Toolkit

To help you continue building on what you've learned, I've created two resources:

1. **The Ultimate GPT Prompt Library:** All the key prompts from this book in a copy-paste format, so you can start using them immediately without flipping through pages.
2. **Join the AI Amplifier Club:** When you're ready to keep the momentum going (with monthly workshops, weekly tactics, proven tools, and a community of action-takers), our core community will help you take the next step.

Both are waiting for you at: AIAdvantage.com/prompt-book.

Index

About the Author

Igor Pogany is Head of Education and partner of AI Advantage and one of the world's leading AI educators, having impacted millions of professionals through his YouTube channel (30M+ views) and hands-on training programs. As an early AI adopter and entrepreneur who has lived in six countries and speaks three languages natively, Igor specializes in translating complex AI capabilities into simple, actionable systems that entrepreneurs can implement immediately. His unique gift: taking what feels overwhelming about AI and making it so clear that anyone, regardless of technical background, can transform how they work.